T0123386

FULL-TIME
SAVIOR

Learning to Trust in Grace

MARCUS BRADLEY

WESTBOW
P R E S S®
A DIVISION OF THOMAS NELSON
& ZONDERVAN

WestBow Press books may be ordered through booksellers or by contacting:

WestBow Press
A Division of Thomas Nelson & Zondervan
1663 Liberty Drive
Bloomington, IN 47403
www.westbowpress.com
1 (866) 928-1240

ISBN: 978-1-5127-4386-9 (sc)
ISBN: 978-1-5127-4385-2 (hc)
ISBN: 978-1-5127-4387-6 (e)

Library of Congress Control Number: 2016908441

Print information available on the last page.

WestBow Press rev. date: 6/6/2016

When I (the author) took the liberty to emphasize certain portions of Scripture, I did it by using ellipses, parentheses, italics, and other various forms of punctuation. I strongly encourage readers to look up all the Bible passages in their perfect form for themselves.

INTRODUCTION

Observation of the Old Testament Law is making a comeback in some Christian circles. A small portion of this book is in response to the movements that are trying to weave the law into policy. Although the general Christian population does not adhere to the law itself, many of us seem to believe in newer forms of law—usually without classifying it as such, and perhaps not even realizing it. Regardless of which type of law embraced, it is quite apparent that the pursuit of religious perfection, dotted with works and rituals, is wiggling its way back into the salvation conversation—or at the very least, popping up in doctrines of right versus wrong.

To put it as plainly as I can, some Christians are reverting back to a rules-based religion that appears to be good and Biblical, but actually centers itself on laws and systems instead of our Savior, Jesus Christ. Although we find "rules" for life in the Bible, all religious instructions are secondary, even meaningless, without these three foundational truths of our Christian faith:

- First and foremost, the only salvation we will ever receive is that of God's grace. We cannot save ourselves, *nor can we supplement our salvation.*
- Secondly, our righteousness is established *entirely* through faith in Jesus Christ (Romans 4:2–5:2). Even though faith without works is dead (James 2:26), the Bible says our righteous acts are like filthy rags (Isaiah 64:6). In other

words, faithful people obviously do good deeds and obey ordinances from Scripture, but those things earn us nothing. Jesus earned everything at the cross.

- And finally, we will never justify ourselves as being good enough before God or man, no matter what we do. It is only by the grace of God through the blood of Christ that we are saved, justified, and declared righteous.

Many of us struggle with the concept of grace, and we instinctively want to play an important role in our own salvation and justification—thus our migration to measurable and definable (and often restricting) laws and rules. But as you will see throughout this book, it is imperative for our individual growth and corporate functionality that we accept God's invitation to a life of spiritual freedom by trusting in the reality of His grace, depending on the blood of His Son, and diving into the depths of His love.

SECTION ONE

1

> For it is by grace you have been saved, *through faith*—and this is not from yourselves, it is the gift of God—not by works, so that no one can boast (Ephesians 2:8–9).

The fact that salvation is a free gift of grace through faith—rather than something we acquire through works—is supposed to be the liberating message of the gospel. But the over-logical can't fathom such grace; the self-sufficient won't accept it; and the self-righteous don't want it.

Combining grace and works is a common practice used by Christians who believe that salvation is a defined, physical occurrence; or by those who believe that personal righteousness is "attainable," at least to some degree. Regardless of the reasoning behind its use, any grace-works combination creates a code of beliefs I call *selective grace,* as opposed to *absolute grace.*

Selective grace is based on the premise that God has a system (instead of, or in addition to Jesus) for us to obey, in order to receive His grace and keep it. Basically, to believe in selective grace is to believe in the notion that we play a tangible role in the activation and retention of grace, rather than trusting fully in Jesus Christ. Absolute grace trusts in the blood of Christ, whereas selective grace is built on theological credos, obedient actions, and other perceived merits.

These kinds of selective grace systems (which vary among our churches) are well-intentioned, but insufficient, attempts to make sense out of God's grace the only way we know how—by humanizing it, systemizing it, and incorporating a set of qualifications for it. But the fundamental problem with systematic grace qualifications is that they don't exist. Grace doesn't have parameters. It doesn't follow rules.

Selective grace implies that you have to qualify for God's grace, one way or another, even if just a little bit. But if you don't believe that grace is unmerited, then you don't believe in it at all.

> If it is by grace, it is no longer on the basis of works, otherwise grace is no longer grace (Romans 11:6 NASB).

It's easy for us to acknowledge grace but awfully tough to trust in it. Grace just seems too simple and effortless, not requiring enough personal responsibility for our own fate. In fact, the marked simplicity of "the gospel of the grace of God" (Acts 20:24 NKJV) has proven to be one of the most challenging things for Christians to believe in. *Our inability to accept God's simple and absolute grace is manifested by our doctrines that keep adding things to it.*

Additions to grace are usually administered by the most religious and self-righteous among us. Although grace is not influenced by human achievement or intellect, the self-righteous—who covet at least a smidgen of credit for the grace that God freely gives—try to manipulate grace, perhaps subconsciously, so they can feel somewhat deserving of it. But grace is a gift from God that is not connected to human deservedness on any level.

The gift of grace is a function of God's heart; and that eliminates all bragging rights from us. Nothing we do—whether individually, corporately, behaviorally or doctrinally—will ever affect grace. *God's grace doesn't care about our best actions or preeminent doctrines, only the blood of Jesus Christ.* So there is no such thing as being good enough or correct enough or deserving in any way. Grace is simpler than that—we either trust Jesus Christ to save us from our sins or we don't.

2

Though it looks very little like it did over a decade ago, this book began as a self-improvement project inspired by 2 Corinthians 13:5. The original goal was to create a physical system that would gauge my heart to see how much it aligned with Jesus. But as the project progressed, it became too complicated. I began to overanalyze myself in every possible way, such that I couldn't do anything without deep, endless introspection. Eventually, I was fortunate enough to realize that no matter how far I go to critique myself or how successful I am at pinpointing and fixing my weaknesses, the forgiveness of my sins through Christ will always be my only hope. *I will never improve enough to eliminate, or even reduce, my need for grace.* This profound truth somewhat destroyed the purpose of my project, yet it was the answer to everything I was looking for. I had finally stumbled upon that elusive, life-changing breakthrough that many Christians never find. For me, it was an emotional experience of the simple gospel that I had been intellectually taught my entire life. This sums it up:

I will never be perfect. But that's okay. Jesus is all I need. *Let Him save me.*

At the point of realizing that Jesus trumps all my improvement efforts, this project took a 180 degree turn. It unexpectedly evolved from aimless scrutiny of self to meaningful pursuit of Christ and His love—because I learned firsthand that self-analysis, religious quests, and good intentions can take me down a million paths, but Jesus Christ will *always* steer me to the gospel, the forgiving love of God.

3

If I have the gift of prophecy and can fathom all mysteries and all knowledge, and if I have a faith that can move mountains, but have not love, I am nothing. If I give all I possess to the poor … but have not love, I gain nothing. Love is patient, love is kind. It does not envy, it does not boast, it is not proud. It is not rude, it is not self-seeking, it is not easily angered, *it keeps no record of wrongs* (1 Corinthians 13:2–5).

There is no bigger source of freedom than to know that God does not keep track of your sins. You are not called to toil throughout your life, trying to be as perfect as possible, hoping the grace of God will cover the balance of your imperfection. In fact, the sole intention of grace is to release you from that kind of life. *The design of grace is to remove every performance burden from you so that you are free to worship God.* To worship God requires the removal of focus from self; therefore, to live a life of worship calls for you to be ever-mindful and grateful for the cross that liberates you, rather than sulking or pouting about the sins you are liberated from.

Grace does not clean up the messes you leave behind; it doesn't even notice you make them. Thanks to Jesus, your sins are not acknowledged, and they never will be. Your past, present, and future sins are completely forgiven. They do not exist in God's eyes. The grace of God is that He *chooses* to see the blood of Christ instead of your transgressions.

By definition, grace leaves a clean slate in its wake; and that never changes. And it's always available—God's grace is ever abundant and His mercies never cease (Lamentations 3:22–23). This grace is so plentiful that it will always be there for you to have, when you obviously need it and when you seemingly don't.

If we get perfectly honest with ourselves, many of us would find that we don't want Jesus to be our 100 percent Savior—maybe 90 percent, but not 100. We would like to think that if we're living well and clean, or perhaps receiving a solid theological education, that it should count for something. We imagine that our spiritual and religious progress have an eternal value. But that's not the way it works. Don't get me wrong—it's important to progress spiritually, live an obedient life, and continuously learn more about God's Word; but those things don't add checkmarks next to your name in the Book of Life. Only Jesus does.

Jesus is your only hope for salvation. He is your only Savior. He is not your safety net or set of training wheels to save you only when you need saving. He is your *Full-Time Savior.* That means your acceptability *never* depends on you. When you drop the ball, God still sees you as righteous, because your sins are filtered through the blood of Jesus Christ that renders you spotless. And likewise, when you're a shining star, God views you as holy, but only because of Jesus. It is the blood of Christ that makes you holy. You're never holy because of you. And thanks to Jesus, you're never unholy because of you.

Neither your strengths nor your weaknesses determine your value. The blood of Jesus is more powerful than anything you do, good or bad. *Your best and worst actions fall together on a straight line somewhere beneath the cross.*

4

Those who make the Christian life more about human righteousness than grace through Jesus Christ are the ones who inadvertently turn holy living into a competition. Living a wholesome life is obviously highly regarded in the Christian faith, but being more holy than others (as an individual or a church) does not affect how God feels about us. Holiness is not a contest or a means of finding favor in any way. It's certainly true that as we grow in the Lord we will become more and more holy, but that doesn't give us extra credit or help determine our approval. The choice to purify our lives is a responsive and voluntary act of love for the Lord, but it doesn't add to our résumés for heaven.

No one will be declared righteous in His sight by observing the law; rather, through the law we become conscious of sin. But now a righteousness from God, apart from law, has been made known, to which the Law and the Prophets testify. *This righteousness from God comes through faith in Jesus Christ to all who believe.* There is no difference (no comparison), for all have sinned and fall short of the glory of God, and are *justified freely by his grace* through the redemption that came by Christ Jesus (Romans 3:20–24).

SECTION TWO

5

First Samuel 30:22–24 is part of a story of how David and his men won a battle and recovered lots of plunder. It's also an example that gives us insight into God's unconventional rewarding system. The synopsis of this passage is that two hundred of David's men dismissed themselves from the tussle before it ever began, because they were too exhausted to fight. After the battle, those who fought bravely didn't want the lazy stragglers to get any of the plunder. But David put a stop to that and declared they would all share alike—even the ones who didn't seem to deserve it.

I believe this passage of Scripture, which is remarkably similar to the parable of the workers in the vineyard (Matthew 20:1–16), exemplifies why God called David a "man after his own heart" (1 Samuel 13:14). According to verses 23–24 of the cited passage, David understood that all the plunder is the Lord's, so he felt there was no reason to wrangle over it. He decided that everyone in his army—regardless of individual roles—should be blessed with the same reward.

Likewise, Christians will not be equally deserving of the gift that awaits us—eternal life—but every one of us will receive it nonetheless. Clearly, God does not operate like we do (Isaiah 55:8–9). Unlike God, we are an insecure, competitive bunch that strives to outperform others. We establish hierarchies of prizes that reward performance—trophies, medallions, and so forth; and some suggest that eternal life is also a reward—a reward for doing things right. But the Bible makes it clear: Heaven is not subject to our reward systems. No one deserves heaven. Eternal life is only possible because of Jesus, and it is a free gift to all who trust in Him.

None of us are righteous, so why argue who's most right? None of us are good, so why debate who's best? None of us deserve heaven, so why compete for it? God does not listen to our logic, but for some reason we still quarrel about things as if He does.

Each Christian denomination, which I loosely define as any group of Christians that has any different beliefs from any other set of believers (that should cover everyone), has at least one distinguishing feature that they boast. These distinctions often escalate from something of *preference* to something of *essence*. And for some, these defining traits mutate from an opinion or a point of view to a matter of urgency that affects salvation.

For the church as a whole, the time has come where the gospel of Jesus can no longer take a backseat to any of the debates that separate us from one another. Division occurs among us whenever it takes more than these three words to sum up our faith—"grace through Jesus." We cannot afford to lose sight of how simple the gospel is. We cannot let people change it from the forgiveness of our sins through Christ to a specific, *correct way* of accepting Him. Nor can we permit the gospel to include details such as spiritual gifts, prophecy, church rituals, or things of that nature. Those things may be good, but they aren't to be attached to the gospel. The gospel is the good news of Jesus Christ and nothing else. *If we let meticulous doctrines become too important, we risk taking our eyes off the cross.* The church cannot allow the role of doctrine to graduate from *supporting* Jesus to *replacing* Him.

The truth is the vast majority of us never argue the actual gospel, whether we realize that or not. Though there are hundreds of Christian movements and dozens of bitter arguments between us, I assume we all agree with this:

> Jesus is the Christ, the Son of the Living God. And because of God's intense love for you, Jesus came to die for you. He is the blood atonement for your sins—the Sacrifice, the Ransom, and the Scapegoat. But first, He was born of a virgin and lived a perfect life without sin. Then He died a horrible death by crucifixion, but He rose from the grave on the third day and subsequently conquered sin and death! And when you accept Jesus as your personal Lord and Savior, your sins are forgiven, and you too conquer death and live eternally.

That's the gospel in a nutshell, and most of us would agree with that. Our debates have never been about the good news of Jesus. The gospel itself does not change and is not argued. We don't squabble over the fact *that* Jesus saves, but we dispute *whom* Jesus saves or *how* Jesus saves or *when* Jesus saves. As these disputes arise, a catastrophic scenario develops that leaves the church unproductive—our differing methods and opinions become more of a focal point than our Savior. Fortunately, or unfortunately, depending on how you see it, there's a perfectly good explanation for all of our debates and tangents:

Human nature competes for God's approval, even when there's no reason to do so. We try to be better than others. We try to gain value by being more Biblically correct than others, even down to the minor details. But approval from God is not about pristine accuracy or following a list of rules or anything else that could physically come from us; it's about the blood of Jesus.

Resist the human tendency to confuse the gospel with the micro-doctrines of man, usually glued together by a few Bible verses from here and there and everywhere. These doctrines that accentuate certain acts and facts can increase our Bible knowledge, which is very important as we grow in the Lord, but it isn't the saving gospel. The gospel is the story of the empty tomb that was designed to hold the bones of Jesus forever, but did not have the power to do so. That is the gospel, and that's why you're saved—because you believe in the empty tomb, you believe Jesus is God, you believe your sins are forgiven through His blood, and you worship and follow and trust Him because of it.

6

Although no one can rightly alter, subtract from, or add to God's Word, they can understand it a little differently. I see things differently than most. I can't help it. I peer through my own lens. That's not good or bad, necessarily; it's just a fact. As I observe most things in life, I take away something that no one else does. And the same is true for you. But oddly enough, when it comes to things like road signs or emergency instructions, I understand them exactly as you do. So how is it that we don't confuse this type of critical information? How do our minds practice some kind of universal comprehension for the absolutes of life? What makes them so unmistakable? Could it be the same phenomenon that helps Christians unequivocally know and believe the *real gospel*, even though we have different takes on so many other things?

It seems to me the only thing truly left untouched in the arguments between our imperfect Christian movements and churches ("imperfect" embodies every movement and every church that has ever existed) is Jesus Christ Himself. In effect, Jesus is our road sign—the one absolute that we don't interpret differently. I know there are some exceptions and offshoots out there, but 99 percent of us understand precisely the role of Jesus Christ as Savior, even though we argue hundreds of other things.

Shouldn't this mean something? Don't you think there's a reason God has protected, in the midst of our endless debates, the name and eternal authority of Jesus Christ, His Son? I don't know all the answers, but maybe it's possible that the gospel story of Jesus Christ and the forgiveness of sins through Him is the only thing that *needs* perfect clarity in the big picture.

Human involvement guarantees distortion. Remember the game many of us played as kids, where one person whispered something to the next person, and that person told their neighbor and so on? People whispered all the way around the table until the message was returned to the original whisperer. I don't recall anyone's initial statement ever coming back to them unchanged. In fact, that was the point of the game—kids found it funny to see how much the sentence changed as it went around the table. Interestingly, we don't realize how much that kids' game reflects adult reality.

Humans distort. We complicate. We confuse. We have selective hearing. We speculate. Our minds convince us that something must be true, even when it's not. Every one of us is guilty of these things. We all distort. I am not immune to distortion or confusion, and neither are you. I am certainly not a human piano that never goes out of tune. No one is. Not me, not you, not your favorite preacher—no one is always in tune. It's simply part of being human.

With distortion as a given, it's also important to note that none of us distort things exactly alike. Our minds take us down individual trains of thought. Our perceptions and viewpoints are not identical. My mind distorts things differently than yours. And there is no *right way* to distort things. There is no person who can be designated as the *instrument of least distortion* by which everyone else should be calibrated. Because of this concept, I cannot consider my church—which is nothing more than a compilation of distorted humans—to be the benchmark for all churches. I cannot perceive those churches and denominations that stray from our beliefs as being out of tune. Because the truth of the matter is that *all* churches are somewhat out of tune.

We should not place stock in our ever-changing Christian movements. Human involvement guarantees that we have distorted things over time. But even though our methods and movements are imperfect and shifting, our Savior is not. Jesus always remains constant (Hebrews 13:8). Fortunately for us, Jesus the Constant says, "I am the Way" (John 14:6). He didn't say our rock-solid doctrines are the way. He didn't say the most accurate church with the least amount of distortion is the way. He said, "*I am* the Way."

7

There are thirteen thousand words (approximately) written about salvation in the New Testament (please refer to the appendix at the end of this book). Our job is not to reduce those words to a list of things that we must do to be saved. Our job is to believe those thirteen thousand words when they tell us that our salvation comes from what Jesus did. The whole point of trusting in Jesus is that we acknowledge we aren't perfect and we believe He can save us. So it's important that our faith and hope are actually in Him—not in a list on how to be saved or a list of our responsibilities of any kind. The old covenant was a list of human requirements. The new covenant is Jesus. The new covenant makes the old one obsolete (Hebrews 8:13; 10:1–10). God did not replace one list with another. He replaced all lists with His Son.

Our ability to interpret the New Testament and deliver an accurate plan of salvation is not what triggers Jesus to save us from our sins. The power of the saving blood of Christ is not bound by any of our methods or interpretations. The power is in the actual blood that was shed on the cross, because there was no blemish in the one who shed it!

I want to clarify that I don't think it's a bad thing to make a list from the Bible (mainly because that indicates we're reading it.) And in the case of salvation, a list could include things like confession, repentance, baptism, etc. Those things are obviously very good. They are clearly Biblical, and we should do what the Bible says. But we just need to make sure that we do not put more faith in the measures that surround salvation than we do in Jesus Christ Himself. We cannot forget that Jesus achieved our salvation for us. It is the blood of Christ that saves us, not something we can do for ourselves. Nothing less than Jesus will ever save us, and nothing more.

The truth is not:

"Jesus saves me, *if I do this or that...*"

The truth is:

"Jesus saves me, period. Therefore, because Jesus saves me, I will put my faith in Him and follow Him to the best of my ability."

8

God alone made it possible for you to be in Christ
Jesus. For our benefit God made Christ to be wisdom
itself. He is the one who made us acceptable to God.
He made us pure and holy, and he gave Himself to
purchase our freedom (1 Corinthians 1:30 NLT).

The fear of trusting in the freedom and grace that we have through
Christ is the force that fastens some Christians to rules and
demands. For these believers, it just doesn't feel right to trust in
anything besides some type of performance-based salvation. This
is true for those who believe in performance (usually of rituals)
to *obtain* salvation or for those who trust in a holy performance to
retain salvation. For the latter group, these people accept Jesus, but
never stop trying to earn their own way, as if they have a bargain
to live up to. Therefore, they never experience the freedom that
we have in Christ. Rather than trusting in Jesus, they trust in a
code of rituals and rules and their ability to flawlessly uphold the
expectations put on them. The truth is they aren't comfortable
enough with Jesus to let go of all the responsibility for their own
salvation and justification. In other words, their faith is not in
Jesus but in themselves. No wonder they live in fear. They're still
trying to save themselves.

Human nature understands fair tradeoffs—things like checks and balances, debits and credits, and paychecks for time served. But God's choice to sacrifice His Son for our salvation was not a fair trade, nor was it supposed to be.

Salvation through Christ is unquestionably designed to be entirely unrelated to any works on our part. And we are to let salvation be what it is—a demonstration of God's irrational and unwarranted love for us, which does not require anything in exchange. We are not to try to make it fit into the box of human reason, which thinks along the lines of getting what you deserve. Human nature wants to be deemed worthy in some small way, even if just for a speck of obedience. But salvation is to believe and accept the sacrifice of Christ as being more than sufficient for you. To put it another way, Jesus is plenty powerful enough to save you; so resist the urge to try to help Him out. You'll only get in the way.

There is only one way to be in God's presence at the end of time—via perfection. *Near perfection means absolutely nothing.* Valiant efforts won't get you a sniff of heaven. This identifies the purpose and importance of trusting in the perfection of Jesus Christ instead of anything that comes from you. Nothing—not good works, not personal holiness, not perfect theology—nothing but Jesus will ever get you to God (1 Timothy 2:5–6).

The day it all clicks—when you let the power of the blood of Christ sink in, when your faith truly shifts from works and theology to Jesus, when you stop trying to earn your way to heaven—that's the day you'll finally be released from the burden of trying to save yourself. And that's what I call the *Salvation Day for the Saved.*

SECTION THREE

9

Jesus didn't have to die on the cross for you. There was nothing for Him to gain by suffering through such brutality and pain—except for your love. And that was enough. That's why He did it. Jesus proved that you are worth *everything* to Him. That is the love of Christ—a willingness to be crucified for you, just for the hope that you will love Him back.

Did it work? Do you love Him?

If you love Me, you will keep My commandments (John 14:15 NASB).

This is My commandment, that you love one another, just as I have loved you (John 15:12 NASB).

A new command I give you: Love one another. As I have loved you, so you must love one another. By this everyone will know that you are my disciples, if you love one another (John 13:34–35).

10

Without a doubt, desire for church unity is a telltale sign of spiritual maturity. However, this desire for unity is not to be confused with a desire to see a massive convergence by all Christians to one precise doctrine. It's not a hope that all denominations will come to their senses and perfectly align their belief systems with mine. *Church unity is not predicated on likeness, but on love; because love overlooks differences* (Colossians 3:11–15; Ephesians 4:1–3; 1 Peter 4:8).

Natural unity is dictated by laws of similarity, but spiritual unity is not. The best example of spiritual unity we have—other than the numerous passages in the New Testament about Jesus being the Savior of the Jews *and* Gentiles, which was unthinkable in those times—is heaven. When we imagine heaven, is it filled with one type of person? Is it occupied by one branch of Christianity? Of course not. It's shallow and foolish to believe that heaven will be made up of millions of people who are just like me. Heaven is not a collection of carbon copies, and it certainly isn't reserved for one sect of Christians. It's a place where *all* believers will congregate with the Lord.

Heaven was created as a direct result of love, which has nothing to do with religious uniformity. God's love is much bigger and much purer than a set of policies and procedures. Therefore, heaven is not a cemetery for the Christians who get everything right. It's not a trophy for those of us with the best argument for it. Heaven is a melting pot of people who place their faith in Jesus Christ and rely on Him for salvation.

11

Church unity is a tough sell, because people are naturally drawn to division. People have always found comfort within their own kind. That's just the way it is. But church unity isn't a physical merger of all Christians—it's a tolerance of them. *The goal is not to be identical, but to unite.*

> Walk in a manner worthy of the calling with which you have been called, with all humility and gentleness, with patience, *showing tolerance for one another in love, being diligent to preserve the unity of the Spirit* (Ephesians 4:1–3 NASB).

> As God's chosen people, holy and dearly loved, clothe yourselves with compassion, kindness, humility, gentleness and patience. Bear with each other and forgive one another if any of you has a grievance against someone. Forgive as the Lord forgave you. *And over all these virtues put on love, which binds them all together in perfect unity.* Let the peace of Christ rule in your hearts, since as members of one body you were called to peace (Colossians 3:12–15).

12

As the apostle Paul wrote his letters to the early Christians, he rarely, if ever, made an entire point in one sentence or one verse. He was incredibly detailed and methodical, purposely penning each sentence to support his overall point. We know he didn't write in chapter-and-verse format, but in today's Bible, his thoughts often take more than one chapter to complete.

A simple example of Paul spending lots of time on one important point was Romans 14:1–15:7. If you take a moment to read that, you will notice that Paul makes it clear that God accepts all types of Christians, even though we have different convictions and practice different rituals—and we are likewise to accept one another for the sake of unity and to bring glory to God. Here is the closing from Paul's lengthy passage:

> May the God who gives endurance and encouragement give you a spirit of unity among yourselves as you follow Christ Jesus, so that with one heart and mouth you may glorify the God and Father of our Lord Jesus Christ. Accept one another, then, just as Christ accepted you, in order to bring praise to God (Romans 15:5–7).

13

If you have any encouragement from being united with Christ, if any comfort from his love, if any fellowship with the Spirit, if any tenderness and compassion, then make my joy complete by being like-minded, *having the same love, being one in spirit and purpose* (Philippians 2:1–2).

Our basic purposes are to worship God and win the lost. We accomplish both of these goals by growing in God's love as individuals and spreading the gospel of grace as the church. God's grace is a manifestation of His love, which is what everyone in the world craves, whether they know it or not. The love of God is irresistible when it's truly experienced; so it's our job as the church to introduce people to it (John 13:34–35), and it's our unity as the body that proves we have it (John 17:20–23).

Church unity occurs when we unconditionally love and accept one another without keeping track of mistakes and differences. This acceptance needs to take place within each congregation, and it also needs to happen within the bigger body of Christ. Our unity at all levels is the only effective way to win the lost. Think about it: Why would the world believe God loves them, if we—who are representatives of God to them—don't love one another; but instead, we point out what's wrong with each other?

Every person who walks through the doors of your church—whether members, regular attendees, or visitors—should feel loved and accepted, by us and by God, as their imperfect self. Accepting people as they are truly frees them up to be themselves, which is the *only* way to experience God's love. This freedom to be real—and still be loved—is the biggest attraction to unbelievers, as it should be. They need to see, believe, and feel that God loves them for who they are. But the thing to keep in mind is that much of their belief in God's love for them will come from the observation of how we treat each other. Do we love each other unconditionally? Do we accept one another, in spite of our differences? The answers to these questions will largely determine our long-term effectiveness as the body of Christ.

14

My purpose is that they may be encouraged in heart and united in love, so that they may have the full riches of complete understanding, in order that they may know the mystery of God, namely Christ, in whom are hidden all the treasures of wisdom and knowledge (Colossians 2:2–3).

Did you catch that? Unity brings full understanding. Until we unite, we won't understand the things that we could. We won't be doing the things that we should, as God's church. There is a treasure chest of wisdom and knowledge that can only be unlocked when we unite as the body of Christ.

It was he who gave some to be apostles, some to be prophets, some to be evangelists, and some to be pastors and teachers, to prepare God's people for works of service, *so that the body of Christ may be built up until we all reach unity in the faith and in the knowledge of the Son of God and become mature, attaining to the whole measure of the fullness of Christ.* Then we will no longer be infants, tossed back and forth by the waves, and blown here and there by every wind of teaching and by the cunning and craftiness of men in their deceitful scheming.

Instead, speaking the truth in love, we will in all things grow up into him who is the Head, that is, Christ. From him the whole body, joined and held together by every supporting ligament, grows and builds itself up in love, as each part does its work (Ephesians 4:11–16).

SECTION FOUR

15

The drive to compete for acceptance is so ingrained in humans that we spend our entire lives doing it. We don't always realize it, but competition is in the fabric of everything we do. We compete for attention, admiration, reputation, promotions, playing time, the lead role, the best grade, social status. We compete for everything; so it's natural to mistakenly feel like we need to compete for God's approval, even the gift of eternal life. But there is no need to compete for a spot in heaven. God doesn't have a finite number of lockers awaiting us. This is not musical chairs where someone is guaranteed to be left out. But that's difficult to grasp because of what we encounter in everyday life. We're so familiar with one "winner" that it's hard to understand that we can all be in heaven.

I certainly used to believe in clear-cut winners for God's approval: "Let's see who wins—my doctrine versus yours. Winner goes to heaven; loser goes to hell." But that's not how it works at all. It's much simpler than that. The way to heaven starts and stops with Jesus. And He knew we'd struggle with this concept. Why else would He tell us to believe like little children if not for our knack of complicating things (Matthew 18:3–4)? And that's exactly what we've done. Many of us now place our faith in things beyond the gospel, beyond Jesus. But let's get back to the truth of the gospel, who is Jesus Christ alone. He is the Beginning and the End, the First and the Last, the Alpha and the Omega

(Revelation 22:13). There is nothing more than Jesus. He is all. He is the Christ, the Son of God. He is the gospel.

Jesus died for all of us, not just the best of us—all of us. And we all can be saved by accepting Him as our Savior and putting our faith in Him. We aren't saved because we deserve it. We aren't saved because we got something right. We aren't saved because of anything we do. If that were so, then Jesus Christ would not be the Savior that He is. If we factored into salvation, then any and all of the competitions between Christians *would* matter. They would be justified. But fortunately, we don't factor into salvation. Therefore, she who has the fewest sins doesn't go to the front of the line for heaven. He who interprets the Bible most accurately doesn't prevail in victory over the rest of us. The point is we must learn to harness our competitive natures so they don't sneak into our spiritual lives and taint our faith in Christ.

I heard a sermon back in 2002 that didn't sit right with my spirit. It was about how we Christians have had several different movements over the last few centuries that have resulted in new denominations with rejuvenated commitments to things that had been lost over the years. I guess that part is fine. But the speaker went on to say there is finally a movement that brings us "full circle." Now we're where we need to be, the speaker said. In other words, he believed the movement of which he was a part was superior to other Christian movements.

Oh how easy it is to get sidetracked. Listen, I understand being passionate about a denomination, a movement, or a specific doctrine. On the surface, I suppose that can be okay; but we need to be careful not to fall into any of these traps:

1. We can feel so good about the teaching of our movement that we think too highly of ourselves or too lowly of others.
2. We can begin to worship the parts of our doctrine that distinguish us.
3. We can become more committed to our specific beliefs than to our Lord.

There is no ultimate sector of Christianity, so don't be ensnared by placing your faith in particular precepts or unique beliefs. Place your faith in Jesus Christ alone.

> Notice what large letters I use as I write these closing words in my own handwriting. Those who are trying to force you to be circumcised (follow laws) are doing it for just one reason. They don't want to be persecuted for teaching that the cross of Christ alone can save … *As for me, God forbid that I should boast about anything* except the cross of our Lord Jesus Christ* (Galatians 6:11–14 NLT).

*In context, Paul was talking about religious boasting, not bragging about a promotion at work or Junior hitting a home run. He was saying, "The cross of Christ alone saves us; so God forbid that I should advertise anything else."

There is nothing to believe in but the cross of Christ. No dogma shed one ounce of blood for you. No rituals or tenets are the Son of God. A perfect belief system from a perfect theology is neither your savior nor mine. Don't get swept away by nice-sounding systems, convincing theories, or holier-than-thou, our-way-is-best religions. Fixate your faith on Jesus, because He is all that matters.

16

We know that heaven will be a congregation of all believers, not just those from carefully selected denominations. I think it's also safe to assume that we will not be segregated in heaven. That is, I don't believe Timothy or Daniel or whoever is running the coat check will say, "Okay, Baptists go over there. Methodists over here. Pentecostals around the corner." That's not going to happen. Furthermore, we know that Jesus wants God's will done on earth as it is in heaven (Matthew 6:10). So if we know that we will not be segregated in heaven, and if we know that Jesus wants God's will done on earth as it is in heaven, and if we know that the church is divided on earth, then shouldn't we give some "undivided" attention to the church's lack of unity?

Our unity is inevitable in heaven, but some Christians daydream about it on earth. These people hunger for God's will on earth as it is in heaven, because they possess a deep longing for heaven itself. Yes, I believe to crave unity is to ache for heaven. The Christians who thirst for the collaboration of the entire body of Christ have matured beyond themselves to see God's bigger plan. They think like Jesus—they desire His body to come together as one and do God's work. And these are the Christians who yearn to stand in the presence of God one day, honored to blend in with the company of His awesome and massive sea of servants.

At the opposite end of the spectrum, there are some Christians who are appalled at the idea of "blending in" with other types of believers. Truth be told, instead of longing for God's will to be done on earth as it is in heaven, instead of wanting the church to unify and become stronger, they get sucked into the prestige of being a limited edition, the top of the line, the exclusive ones who have it all figured out. They don't want to unite. In fact, they see unity as an insult; because they believe they've distinguished themselves from other Christians—whether in deed or doctrine—which is very important to them. To these elitist Christians, the lure of exclusivity apparently supersedes the consequences of church division. But to be fair, I don't believe they are *choosing* to be a dividing force—I think it's less a matter of choice than identity. I believe the concept of barrier-busting unity destroys the ground they walk on, because their identity is not solely in Christ, but also in the walls that stand between them and other Christians. In other words, their identity is largely tied to differentiation—the things that set their version of Christianity apart from the rest. And where identities are not in Christ alone, people naturally thrive on church division—rejecting the notion of unity—in order to preserve comfort, ego, and "rightness".

These divisive ways of thinking that are so common today can be overcome; and, in fact, they *must* be overcome for the church to fulfill its potential and represent the body of Christ on earth.

Besides the obvious—human nature—what makes it so easy for our thoughts to deviate so far from God's agenda for His church that we get tripped up before we ever begin His work; such that we can't even universally agree on who constitutes the church in the first place? Do we not know that Jesus Christ and the grace we have through Him is the same hope for each of us? Why do we forget—or perhaps dismiss—the basis of our faith? Why does our common ground seem to get lost in the ruins of some splintered maze of detailed religion that we claim to be Christianity?

Legalism is an attempt to gain approval through a righteousness that comes from obeying rules, rather than the righteousness that comes through faith in Jesus Christ. This practice of legalism *always* leads to elitism within the faith. The hallmark of elitism is to believe that certain righteous rules and doctrines make some Christians more worthy than others. Simply put, Christian elitists think their way is better than yours.

Usually centering themselves on doctrinal knowledge, or sometimes believing they are the most "spiritual," elitists ignore the reality that none of us deserve to be called children of God; and they seem to imagine a world in which it matters who *most* deserves it. Basically, they believe their doctrines and actions are worth something. But they aren't.

In essence, legalists and elitists believe (and some of them seem to hope) that the measure to which we perform is more powerful than God's grace. So they perceive and proclaim their excellent achievements, spotless theologies, and quest for human righteousness or spirituality as being valuable, making them (or their wing of Christianity) more superior to others. They refuse to acknowledge the fact that grace makes all Christians equal. To put it kindly, equality bothers them. But grace is, without a doubt, the ultimate equalizer. The gospel of grace is partial to no one. There is no ranking system among humans that could possibly influence grace through Christ. The good news of the gospel is the same for the horribly imperfect as it is for the near perfect: *You both qualify for God's grace.*

SECTION FIVE

17

God is love (1 John 4:8, 16), and love keeps no record of wrongs (1 Corinthians 13:5). Therefore, God doesn't keep record of *anybody's* wrongs, because He loves us all. So when it comes to extending grace or declaring righteousness, God isn't looking for right versus wrong, because He doesn't keep track of wrongs. *He's looking for Jesus.* Where you spend eternity depends on your acceptance of Jesus Christ, not how right or wrong you've been.

> What does the Lord require of you? ... to love
> mercy and to walk humbly (Micah 6:8).

Do you walk humbly? Better yet, *do you love mercy?* How can you quantify that? Well, mercy is a derivative of grace that comes directly from the heart of God; and it's pretty easy to measure—mercy is the part of love that keeps no record of wrongs (1 Corinthians 13:5). With that in mind, are you merciful? Are you quick to forgive? And after pardoning someone, do you let it go? Or do you keep record of wrongs?

18

The inability to forgive is the root of many problems that hinder the church today. Where forgiveness is lacking, things like judgmentalism and perfectionism are thriving. But ultimately, it does no good to talk about fixing the church's lack of mercy on a corporate level when the church is made up of individuals. So I declare that the church's lack of forgiveness—which creates the environment for legalism, elitism, and all the other church-destroying "isms"—is an individual problem that starts with me and you. Surprisingly, our forgiveness deficiency is not so much from the inability to forgive others as it is the inability to forgive oneself.

In the gospels, Jesus says that we ought to forgive others *so we can receive forgiveness* (Mark 11:25–26). But wait a second; aren't we freely forgiven without any strings attached? Yes we are; but we're expected to forgive others in that same way.

So which one comes first—my forgiveness of others or God's forgiveness of me?

The fact of the matter is you can only forgive others after you learn to forgive yourself, because you can't practice more forgiveness than you've experienced. So it is absolutely critical to grasp God's forgiveness of you; because then you'll learn how, and understand why, to forgive yourself. Then, by default, you will learn how to forgive others, too.

The following paragraphs illustrate how forgiveness should work:

Consider what happens when you fall down and scuff your knee. There's usually an instant shot of pain that subsides rather quickly. After that initial pain, you gather yourself, scrub the dirt out, apply peroxide and a bandage, and then let time heal it. I believe this physical example parallels the spiritual world. Repentance is a decision to get back up after you've fallen. Healing starts by cleansing the wound. Covering your heart with God's love and comfort helps minimize your exposure to more pain. Repenting, cleansing, healing, preventing future injury....

"But aren't we talking about forgiveness?" you might ask. "Where does that take place in the illustration?"

After you fall and scrape your knee, your attention immediately goes to your injury. You get up, tend to the wound, and go on about your day. You don't sit on the ground pondering how you shouldn't have fallen—and that's forgiveness. *To forgive yourself is to accept the fact that you fell down.* That's how God forgives you. He accepts you and forgives you for falling, even as you fall. Our entire faith is built on such forgiveness. We have to learn to imitate the grace of God and automatically forgive ourselves with complete acceptance and understanding. And once we do, we will routinely accept others and forgive them for their shortcomings too.

Those who have been forgiven much love much (Luke 7:47). In other words, those who grasp how much they've been forgiven are so grateful for it that they willingly and eagerly forgive others in that same fashion—completely. But those who hold grudges against someone else have yet to accept God's forgiveness themselves.

For those who cling to God's mercy and believe in it wholeheartedly, there is freedom—because knowing the merciful heart of God allows them to instantly forgive themselves and others. But if you do not believe, depend on, and practice God's mercy, then you are not free. In fact, it's utterly impossible to be free if you do not forgive. You are a prisoner to any grudges you have. You are held captive by whomever you cannot forgive. *You are detained and held hostage by anyone's imperfections that you dwell on, including your own.*

Perfectionism is bondage. I not only lived in that bondage in the past, but I attempted to force those closest to me to live in it with me. Why would I do that? Because I wanted to be able to love them. *But since the only way I knew how to love myself is if I was perfect, the only way I knew how to love them is if they were perfect.*

19

The biggest spiritual freedom you'll ever feel is when you finally *believe* you aren't expected to be perfect anymore. There will be no more cringing in fear from your imperfections. No more replaying the mistakes of your past through your mind. No more hiding from reality. No more living a lie. No more fighting the feelings of rejection. No more desperate attempts for the approval of the ones you always needed it from.

Once you stop beating yourself up for being imperfect, once you learn to truly rest in God's grace, then you'll finally be able to appreciate that God made you who you are on purpose. And once you are free to be yourself, you'll be free to let others be themselves.

When you learn to accept the things about yourself that you don't like, you learn three things:

(1) The nature of God's love, which doesn't see your flaws;
(2) How to overlook things in others; and
(3) How not to be consumed with negatives.

When we sit around thinking about all the bad things in the world or all the things that people do wrong, we develop a negative spirit. This negativity steals our joy and robs us of life. We only get one shot on earth; please don't waste it being negative.

Before Saul's conversion to Paul, he was certainly the type of person that found faults in everything. Acts 8:3 (NASB) says he was "ravaging" the church, going house to house searching for people to imprison for practicing Christianity. It's as if his own faith centered on finding people who didn't believe like him, people he could accuse of wrongdoing. He was completely focused on the negatives, looking for faults in others. But years later, the apostle Paul, who had become an ambassador for Jesus Christ, penned Philippians 4:8:

> Whatever is true, whatever is noble, whatever is *right*, whatever is pure, whatever is lovely, whatever is admirable—if anything is excellent or praiseworthy—think about such things.

Nowhere does Paul say to dwell on the bad. Nowhere does Paul say to pinpoint the errors in everyone's ways. Quite the contrary: he said to think about good things. *He said to think about what is right, not what is wrong.* Paul learned how to let the Holy Spirit change his way of thinking, and so can we.

SECTION SIX

20

College football coaches have to change with the times to appeal to recruits. They must be willing to adapt to the evolution of the athletes. There are some principles to keep forever, but they need to frequently tweak their styles and strategies so they can attract great players and continue to win.

The changes in football over the years are a microcosm of the world. Everything changes but change itself. Times change; people change; and churches change too. Your church may be like it was two years ago, twenty years ago, or maybe even two hundred years ago, but no church is how it was two thousand years ago. And the way you prefer things to be—as they are today or how they used to be—is a result of change, even if that change was made a century ago.

Whether we like it or not, the church is an evolving product for an evolving market, just like it's always been. The design of a church building or the structure of a worship service has no industry standard, other than leading souls to Jesus. It might not make sense for your church to radically change styles in order to reel in a whole new crowd; but within the body of Christ as a whole, there must be diverse church options so we can appeal to *all* types of people. And we can't let ourselves look down on one another based on any of these church differences. It's simply unreasonable to expect everyone to be alike, and it's somewhat indicting on those who *want* everyone to be alike.

To be clear, traditional churches can't frown on the modern ones that target a different generation. At the same time, progressive churches can't view the traditionalists as "not getting it." Both kinds of churches play pivotal roles in God's kingdom.

Ultimately, we should allow for some variety. It can be hard to accept different styles and points of view. But it's important, in the big picture, to try—because "the big picture" is not about personal preferences, but converting lost souls.

21

Human nature wants to make the human role more important than it is. Therefore, we naturally compare ourselves to others with the hopes that we measure up favorably. These comparisons trickle into our faith, which lead us to assess other strands of Christianity in a competitive spirit. With eternity seemingly at stake (a trick our minds play on us when we evaluate the practices of other Christians), arguments develop over things such as "how to be holy," as if our actions and creeds matter, or "how to be saved," as if we can save ourselves.

When we forget that Jesus alone makes us holy, we start puffing chests and pointing fingers. When we forget that Jesus alone is our Savior, we clutch tighter to our micro-doctrines and drift apart. And when we forget that the body of Christ needs all its parts to efficiently operate together (Ephesians 4:11–16), we become less effective in achieving the agenda of Christ, which is to "seek and save the lost" (Luke 19:10).

As denominations of Christianity become more critical of one another, we become more focused on our differences than on Jesus. As our eyes wander away from the cross, such that Jesus Himself is no longer the center, we quickly succumb to church division. And as the church fragments into hundreds of shards, our strength diminishes and our usefulness wanes. That's why one of Satan's chief tactics is to divide us on a church level (not to mention a family level); and often times, from there he tries to isolate us into little groups cut off from the bigger kingdom of God.

If Christians were becoming more like Christ, we would be coming closer together instead of remaining so divided. But in order to come together and be like Jesus, we have to understand that it's not what we do that makes us more like Christ—it's who we are. What we do shouldn't divide us. Who we are should unite us.

The arguments among Christians will stop when we zero in on the *heart* of Jesus. We all know who Jesus is and believe He's God in the flesh. We accept His teachings and what He stood for. We all claim Him as our personal Lord and Savior. But for some reason, the arguments within the faith never end.

These things we contend about—such as musical preferences, whether certain spiritual gifts "are for today," interpretations about the end times, and other secondary things such as these— are ultimately pointless. To me, once we accept Christ as Lord of our life, the things of importance are the fruits of the Spirit listed in Galatians 5; because once those traits become the core of who we are, then we will be becoming more like Jesus through the power of the Holy Spirit. And as we grow individually in the Spirit, all of our disagreements should dissipate; because the things we argue about have nothing to do with what the Spirit cares about. The work of the Holy Spirit (building the church into the image of Christ) is a single-minded operation with a very specific target—your heart.

The rate of growth in Christ through the Spirit will vary among believers, so toss the notion aside that you are to judge yourself or someone else based on any outward proof of the fruits of the Spirit. Mental measuring sticks are unimportant, even if they are obvious. The only true objective, on an individual level, for the rest of your life, is to pursue Jesus with all of your heart, and not just your head. And as you seek Him, the Holy Spirit will certainly produce His fruits inside of you (2 Corinthians 3:16–18). The way to assist the Spirit in this process is to train yourself to care more about *who to be* (heart, spirit) than *what to do* (head, flesh).

As we develop into people who reflect the heart of Jesus, our judgmental natures will fade away and our silly debates will diminish. That's because things will start becoming less about us and our ways of *doing*, and more about Jesus and His way of *being*.

22

I believe our church unity, much like our salvation, has nothing to do with effort. It's not a physical or tangible event. Unity cannot be forced. It's not a movement or a conscious decision. Unity is an automatic response to the love of Christ, a byproduct of personal growth in the Lord.

Theoretically, as we grow in God's love, our hearts will begin to consistently align with Jesus. And as we become more like Him, we'll start to desire what He does. To see His heart exposed for ourselves, we can read the last Biblical reference to a prayer from Jesus (John 17), which took place moments before the arrest that led to His crucifixion. As Jesus was about to bear the weight of the world on His shoulders—at the moment where He felt more stress than anyone else has ever felt before or will ever feel again—He pleaded to God from His heart. And of all the things to be on the heart of our Savior at the most pressure-packed point of His life, at the climax of human history, this is what Jesus was thinking about:

> My prayer is ... that all (who believe in me) may be one ... May they be brought to complete unity to let the world know that you sent me and have loved them even as you have loved me (John 17:20–23 NLT).

According to the text, the unity of the believers weighed so heavily on Jesus because unity is what proves to the world that He is God's Son and that God loves them. We are the body of Christ, and we are indeed the ones to spread God's love to the world today. That's why Jesus longs for us to unify through love—He needs us to *be Him*, the One Son of God, to the unbelievers. And since we pursue the heart of Christ, don't we also burn inside with this desire to unify and become Christ to the world?

It's difficult to imagine a physical unity of one church on earth, but there is a practical possibility that I find great hope in. By way of analogy, if everyone decided to simultaneously go to the heart of America—say, Kansas City—then as we traveled from all directions, we would keep getting closer and closer to each other. In a similar way, if we all converged on the heart of Christ, the distance between us would naturally shrink. It's not that we'd choose to unite, necessarily. It's just a straightforward truth: the closer we get to Jesus individually, the more we'll come together collectively—because each of our hearts will be heading to the same place.

23

Church unity starts at the individual level, but so does church division. You cannot allow yourself to be a supporter of division by taking pride in being "different than." Healthy self-confidence is dependent on knowing that you are God's standard for you; but you must remember that you are no one else's standard. You are valued for who you are, but everyone else is valued for who they are. There are no comparisons to make, and that's what spells trouble for many individuals, and it certainly wreaks havoc on the church.

People compare themselves to others because they are looking for ways to stand out or find value. But what makes you (or me) different from others is exactly what makes them different from you—personal uniqueness. The individual traits that differentiate us are not to become sources of pride, nor are they reason to panic. It's natural for our distinctions to make us one of two things: arrogant or paranoid. But it's important to be neither. You must be okay with you, independent of comparisons, trusting that God did not make a mistake with you. Not that you are His best piece of art, such that you fetch higher status than others, but that you are the only individual who can play your specific role in God's kingdom. In order to fulfill your personal role in the body of Christ, you must be yourself while allowing others to be themselves.

And the same goes for our churches. Each church has a unique assignment. Comparisons can only be harmful. What makes your church different is not a reason to be conceited. What makes your church different merely defines its role in God's kingdom.

We don't have to agree on everything to unite, just Jesus. We don't have to worship in the same church building or within the same denomination to unite. In order to unite, all we have to do is admit we're on the same team. We all believe in the same Jesus and rely on the same grace, and that's what makes us teammates.

The blood of Jesus pumps through the whole body and gives life to each part. Let us always remember that Christ alone is the heartbeat. And if we keep ourselves glued to Jesus, relying on His blood for life, trusting Him to be the heartbeat of His church, and focusing on Him as the center of the body, then we will be acting in unison, working together, and strengthening Christianity in our communities around the globe. And isn't that the goal? On the contrary, if we take our eyes off of Jesus, we will divide and weaken; because, without Christ, human nature draws our thoughts onto our differences, and we clump together accordingly. But comparing our differences and dividing over them is not a behavior that is condoned by the Holy Spirit. In fact, it's in direct opposition of Him—it's a function of the flesh.

Truth is not found in what separates us, but rather in who unites us. It's easy to be so preoccupied with the differences that divide us that we become blind to the blood of Christ that binds us. We must remember that a united church in Christ wins the lost (John 17:21–23), but a divided kingdom will not stand (Matthew 12:25). That's why the Spirit longs for our unity (Ephesians 4:2–6); and those who live in the Spirit want what the Spirit wants (Romans

8:5). So if we don't really care about being the one body that we are, if we prefer division, then we're living in the flesh and clearly more concerned about being comfortable than saving lost souls.

Christians have to learn to live in the Spirit, set aside denominational differences and personal agendas, and come together. The church has to tout the Savior of the world instead of its differentiating policies. We, the body of Christ, have to keep our eyes on Jesus instead of our creeds, and serve Him instead of the fine print. We cannot afford to become (or remain) clusters of Pharisees; we have to live according to our purpose, which is to reflect the heart of Christ as people, and unify in Him as the body, and win lost souls for Him as the church.

SECTION SEVEN

24

We are informed in Acts 15 of how simple we are to make it for those who turn to the Lord. This passage is a story of how Paul and Barnabas went to Jerusalem to speak with the council of elders and apostles, which included Peter and James, among others, about the fact that some teachers were complicating salvation. Some were even trying to force Jewish customs onto the Gentiles, which should have never happened. But since it did, the Gentiles became confused, and they wanted some clarification. And this is how the original Christian elders responded:

After much discussion, Peter got up and addressed them:

> Brothers, you know that some time ago God made a choice among you that the Gentiles might hear from my lips the message of the gospel and believe. God, who knows the heart, showed that he accepted them by giving the Holy Spirit to them, just as he did to us. He did not discriminate between us and them, for he purified their hearts *by faith*. Now then, why do you try to test God by putting on the necks of Gentiles a yoke that neither we nor our ancestors have been able to bear (the law)? No! We believe it is through the grace of our Lord Jesus that we are saved, just as they are (Acts 15:7–11).

When they finished, James spoke up:

> It is my judgment, therefore, that we should not make it difficult for the Gentiles who are turning to God (Acts 15:13, 19).

Then the apostles and elders sent the following letter to the Gentile believers:

> It seemed good to the Holy Spirit and to us not to burden you with anything beyond the following requirements: You are to abstain from food sacrificed to idols, from blood, from the meat of strangled animals and from sexual immorality. You will do well to avoid these things. Farewell (Acts 15:23, 28–29).

The simplicity of the gospel is falling to the wayside. Many of us have exchanged it for a more complicated product—one with a human element, a human salvation. But nothing of that sort exists. Salvation is not physical. It's not human. It's grace through Christ.

It's natural for us to add to the gospel, but we really need to let it be as simple as it is—there's nothing we can do to help seal our salvation, because once we accept Jesus, the Holy Spirit seals it for us.

> When you believed (in Jesus), you were marked in him with a seal, the promised Holy Spirit,

who is a deposit guaranteeing our inheritance (Ephesians 1:13–14).

It is the Spirit that gives eternal life. Human effort accomplishes nothing (John 6:63 NLT).

25

John 3:16 tells us the truth plainly: "For God so loved the world that he gave his one and only Son, that whoever believes in him shall not perish but have eternal life."

God loves us so much that He gave His *Son*—not more lists of rules and laws, but His Son. So that if we believe in Him, we will have eternal life.

> For the law was given through Moses; (but) grace and truth came through Jesus Christ (John 1:17).

If the law could have given us new life, we could have been made right with God by obeying it. But the Scriptures have declared that we are all prisoners of sin, so the only way to receive God's promise is to believe in Jesus Christ. Until faith in Christ was shown to us as the way of becoming right with God, we were guarded by the law. We were kept in protective custody, so to speak, until we could put our faith in the coming Savior. Let me put it another way. The law was our guardian and teacher to lead us *until Christ came*. So now, through faith in Christ, we are made right with

God. But now that faith in Christ has come, we no longer need the law (Galatians 3:21–25 NLT).

God made you alive in Christ. He forgave us all our sins, *having canceled the written code, with its regulations* ... He took it away, nailing it to the cross. And having disarmed the powers and authorities, he made a public spectacle of them, triumphing over them by the cross. Therefore do not let anyone judge you by what you eat or drink, or with regard to a religious festival, a new-moon celebration or a Sabbath day. These are a shadow of the things that were to come; the reality, however, is found in Christ (Colossians 2:13–17).

You who once were far away have been brought near through the blood of Christ. For he himself is our peace ... by abolishing in his flesh the law with its commandments and regulations (Ephesians 2:13–15).

We have been released from the law so that we serve in the new way of the Spirit, and not in the old way of the written code (Romans 7:6).

Let me ask you this one question: Did you receive the Holy Spirit by keeping the law? Of course not, for the Holy Spirit came upon you only after you believed the message you heard about Christ. Have you lost your senses? After starting your Christian lives in the Spirit, why are you now trying to become perfect by your own human effort? (Galatians 3:2–3 NLT).

You are trying to find favor with God by what you do or don't do on certain days or months or seasons or years. I fear for you. I am afraid that all my hard work for you was worth nothing. Dear brothers and sisters, I plead with you to live as I do in freedom from these things (Galatians 4:10–12 NLT).

I make myself guilty if I rebuild the old system I already tore down. For when I tried to keep the law, I realized I could never earn God's approval. *So I died to the law so that I might live for God.* I have been crucified with Christ. I myself no longer live, but Christ lives in me. So I live my life in this earthly body by trusting in the Son of God, who loved me and gave himself for me. I am not one of those who treats the grace of God as meaningless. For if we could be saved by keeping the law, then there was no need for Christ to die (Galatians 2:18–21 NLT).

You are not under law but under grace (Romans 6:14 NASB).

Your hearts should be strengthened by God's grace, not by obeying rules (Hebrews 13:9 NCV).

I know what enthusiasm they have for God, but it is misdirected zeal. They don't understand God's way of making people right with himself. Instead, they are clinging to their own way of getting right with God by trying to keep the law. They won't go along with God's way. For Christ has accomplished *the whole purpose* of the law. All who believe in him are made right with God (Romans 10:2–4 NLT).

It is clear, then, that God's promise ... to Abraham and his descendants was not based on obedience to God's law, but on the new relationship with God that comes by faith. So if you claim that

God's promise is for those who obey God's law and think they are good enough in God's sight, then you are saying that faith is useless. And in that case, the promise is also meaningless (Romans 4:13–14 NLT).

What does the Scripture say? "Throw out the slave woman and her son. The son of the slave woman should not inherit anything. The son of the free woman should receive it all" [see Genesis 21:10]. So, my brothers and sisters, we are not children of the slave woman, but of the free woman. We have freedom now, because Christ made us free. So stand strong. Do not change and go back into the slavery of the law. Listen, I Paul tell you that if you go back to the law … Christ does you no good (Galatians 4:30–5:2 NCV).

SECTION EIGHT

26

> I will give you a new heart and put a new spirit in you; I will remove from you your heart of stone and give you a heart of flesh (Ezekiel 36:26).

> For it is God who works in you to will and to act according to his good purpose (Philippians 2:13).

God softens and changes your heart. He puts a new spirit in you. He is at work inside of you. And since God is the one who does it, take the pressure off yourself. It's not your job to create your new heart. But at the same time, you must let God facilitate these changes in your life.

When you accept Jesus, the Holy Spirit will change you (2 Corinthians 3:18). You will undergo a lifelong transformation to be made more like Him (Philippians 1:6). So be ready for God to change you and mold you. Trust that He knows what He's doing as He alters you on the inside and shuffles your surroundings on the outside. Embrace the changes of life as part of an adventure with God. Everything that happens in your life is meant to give God glory while simultaneously changing your heart to become more like His, as you get closer to Him every day.

> And we know that God causes all things to
> work together for good to those who love God
> (Romans 8:28 NASB).

Did you notice, in the above verse, that it's God who makes things work out for you? When you try to control everything around you, you interfere with Him. Just settle down. Don't worry about everything. Relax. *God has your best interests at heart.* In fact, He knows them better than you.

God's way takes the elevator to the ninetieth floor. Our way takes the stairs. But sometimes when we don't know exactly what God is doing, we decide to stick with the stairs. That way we can always see right in front of us, every step we take. Even though God's way is the elevator and has less resistance and takes us to our destination smoothly, some of us are reluctant to follow God's way if we can't see where it goes—if we're not in control.

27

It is not good to have zeal without knowledge,
nor to be hasty and miss the way (Proverbs 19:2).

It's hard not to rush in today's world, but we must be patient as we wait for God. For example, if you're full of zeal and passion about something, that doesn't necessarily indicate that it's time to start moving. Enthusiasm doesn't mean you know what to do or when to do it.

Recalling my early days in the faith, I remember being pumped full of excitement—but I hadn't yet learned how to wait. I didn't realize that I wasn't quite ready for the things I was excited about. As I tried to get ahead of God, my lack of sturdiness was quickly exposed. I didn't yet have the foundation that God wanted me to have, although I thought I did. The problem was I didn't want to believe how long it takes. I remember saying, "I refuse to limit God or myself with time." Well, if God had wanted to equip me with a full foundation in a month, He could have. But that's not how He operates. He builds. He progresses.

He who gathers … little by little makes it grow
(Proverbs 13:11).

Your beginnings will seem humble, so prosperous
will your future be (Job 8:7).

Wait for God and His timing. Let Him build you over the long haul. Don't try to get ahead of Him. Eliminating haste could be the most important thing to learn in your daily life.

28

No two people learn exactly alike. We're all taught in different ways. That's because none of us have the exact combination of personality, life experience, genetic makeup, etc. And that explains the age-old mystery as to why no one else's brain seems to work like mine. Actually, I was at some point in my twenties when I realized that all brains work differently. It's not exactly common for people to see patterns in their mind, regardless of what they're looking at—from phone numbers to wood grains. But that's what I do. I can't help it. And it's these kinds of nuances that assist my learning. But chances are that's not how you learn. Rumor has it that some people don't care about patterns and don't need every detail; they are able to live with the basic gist of things—and somehow survive! I guess I just always imagined everyone saw things how I saw them, thought how I thought, and learned how I learned. But I was wrong. We all learn differently. We are individuals in every way.

When I gave myself to God and sought Him in spirit and truth, He taught me in ways in which I learn best. By utilizing my natural methods of learning, the Holy Spirit increased my understanding. Similarly, since others learn differently, I realized I had to accept their ways of learning as being sufficient for them. I can't try to force what I learn and how I learn onto others. By the same token, I can't let someone else force their thinking onto me.

Though it would be foolish not to accept sound teaching and direction, we shouldn't blindly carbon copy someone else's beliefs; because that takes the *personal* out of our personal relationship with Jesus. When God teaches us in the ways we learn best, our faith becomes uniquely branded, not generic. We should all come to similar conclusions, but everything is more alive when you learn for yourself through the Spirit and get to know Jesus on a personal level.

Whenever I speak of a personal relationship with Jesus, I'm not referring to an education that teaches you *about* Him. Education is only preparation, not the real thing. Case in point: actually being married is entirely different than being taught about marriage. Another example is that high school and college are designed to prepare you for the real world, but scholastic education does not simulate the job you find when you enter the workforce. Likewise, learning about your Savior is good; but it's not a substitute for Him and it will never replicate a relationship with Him.

Back in the first century, the Pharisees had the best education available, and they hung their hats on that. Today's Pharisees among us do the same. Their educational knowledge is great, but do they know Jesus? Many of them can't fathom what a relationship with Christ is other than religious knowledge. They don't understand what it means to get to a next-level, beyond-knowledge, beyond-doctrine relationship with their Savior.

If you want to get to know Jesus on a more personal level, then tell Him just that. Say something like this: "Jesus, come to me. I want to know You, Lord. I want to pursue a stronger relationship with You." He will oblige.

SECTION NINE

29

Sometimes it's necessary to deconstruct everything of religion that you've known and built, so you can reconstruct yourself in God's love. You can't successfully use the love of God as some kind of filler. Love is not a bandage or asphalt sealant. You don't use love as a patch or a substance to pour over your heart to fill in the cracks. God's love is the foundation:

> I pray that you, *being rooted and established in love*, may have power, together with all the saints, to grasp how wide and long and high and deep is the love of Christ, and to know this love that surpasses knowledge (Ephesians 3:17–19).

It seems that many of us fluctuate between "God loves me so much" and "I'm a complete failure." Bouncing between spiritual poles like this is commonly found among those who put most of their eggs in the basket of personal performance or religious knowledge instead of God's unwavering love for them and the grace they have through Christ. Although God's grace and love are constant, it doesn't feel that way to the spiritually manic. They only accept God's love when it seems like He *should* love them, if they feel like they've earned it. Therefore, as performance oscillates, so does their confidence—confidence in salvation, in God's love for them, in everything. Their self-assurance is based—at least in those moments—on personal performance instead of Jesus Christ.

If you try to make yourself right with God through any source other than faith in Jesus, you will experience unnecessary ups and downs in your spiritual life. And as you ride the yo-yo, it will take everything inside of you to believe in God's mercy; because on good days it will seem like you don't need it and bad days like He doesn't have enough of it. But the truth is God always sees you the same through His steady eyes of mercy, regardless of whether you're up or down, highly deserving or utterly failing.

The key to spiritual health is to rely on God's grace, independently of your performance. It doesn't matter whether you've recently struggled or excelled—know that you are consistently and absolutely loved every day, because that's just who God is.

God not only loves you, *He likes you*. And though He likes you, that's not why He loves you. He loves you because He wants to. Because He dreamed you up. That's why you exist—so God can love you and so you can love Him. You aren't here because of a random combination of genes. You're here because God *wants* you to be here. You're here to receive His love—and to give it back.

> Dear friends, we should love each other, because love comes from God. Everyone who loves has become God's child and knows God. Whoever does not love does not know God, because God is love … This is what real love is: It is not our love for God; it is God's love for us. He sent his Son to die in our place to take away our sins. Dear

friends, if God loved us that much we also should love each other. No one has ever seen God, but if we love each other, God lives in us, and his love is made perfect in us (1 John 4:7–12 NCV).

For God is not unjust. He will not forget … *how you have shown your love to him by caring for other believers* (Hebrews 6:10 NLT).

30

Our top priority as Christians is plainly spoken in 1 Corinthians 14:1 (NLT):

> Let love be your highest goal.

Does it get any clearer than that? Our highest goal is love. Such a claim is consistent with what Jesus told us when He said the greatest commandments are to love God and each other (Matthew 22:37–40). It is no accident that we have countless other New Testament passages that emphasize the importance of love. In fact, the apostle Paul, who was given the responsibility to spread the gospel of grace to the Gentiles (Acts 20:24; Galatians 1:11–16; Ephesians 3:7–8), says that love sums all our rules up into one (Galatians 5:14; Romans 13:8–9). John, who wrote five New Testament books and was part of Jesus' inner circle, proclaims that "God is love" (1 John 4:8, 16). And since love *defines* God, the pursuit of God's love is pursuing God Himself; which could explain why Paul said nothing is greater than love.

> There are three things that will endure—faith, hope, and love—and the greatest of these is love (1 Corinthians 13:13 NLT).

31

As we live in God, our love grows more perfect.
So we will not be afraid on the day of judgment,
but we can face him with confidence ... because
perfect love expels all fear (1 John 4:17–18 NLT).

The love of God, manifested at the cross, grants us the gift of complete confidence on the Day of Judgment. There is nothing to fear—in this world or the next—because Love sent Jesus to overcome the world, which He absolutely did (John 16:33–17:3); and that makes *you* more than a conqueror, inseparable from the love of God (Romans 8:31–39), who is faithful beyond all measure (2 Timothy 2:13).

Fear and faith are polar opposites. They have an inverse relationship: as one increases, the other decreases. So, for Christians, an increasing faith in God (and His love) shrinks our fears.

In God I trust, I will not be afraid (Psalm 56:4).

Surely God is my salvation; I will trust and not be afraid (Isaiah 12:2).

Do not let your hearts be troubled and do not be afraid (John 14:27).

Do not be afraid, for I am with you (Genesis 26:24).

Do not fear; I will help you (Isaiah 41:13).

Fear not, for I have redeemed you (Isaiah 43:1).

Don't be afraid; just believe (Mark 5:36).

SECTION TEN

32

Life in Christ is not to be another burden filled with endless dos and don'ts. Life with Jesus unloads the weight of perfection so you can take on each day without fear, without anxiety, and without pressure to live up to impossibly high expectations.

> Come to me, all you who are weary and burdened, and I will give you rest. Take my yoke upon you and learn from me, for I am gentle and humble in heart, and you will find rest for your souls. For my yoke is easy and my burden is light (Matthew 11:28–30).

In contrast to living in the restful spirit of Christ, there is a life in the religious flesh that is enslaved to the mind, where focus is always on self and how to become better for God. But God doesn't need you to be better. That way of thinking is what creates the lie that self-righteousness is eternally significant. That mindset doesn't grasp God's grace and it demands the highest level of performance, *subconsciously reducing the role of the cross.*

As Christians, we're called to be humble, which is opposite of self-righteous. We're called to glorify and elevate Jesus and *His* holiness, not ours. To quote John the Baptist from John 3:30:

> "[Jesus] must become greater; I must become less."

Of course we want to be good. Of course we want to do better. Of course we want to be more like Jesus every day. But our Christianity, our livelihoods, and our self-assurance do not hinge upon our success, because our hope is in Christ. We can't obsess with how badly we want to be good. We've got to keep everything about Jesus, and we've got to keep our hope in God's grace through Him.

We can have full confidence that the Holy Spirit will help us get better (2 Corinthians 3:18; Philippians 1:6), but we put no confidence in how good we actually are.

> We put no confidence in human effort. Instead
> we boast about what Christ Jesus has done for us
> (Philippians 3:3 NLT).

Jesus Christ assumes full responsibility for you because He accomplished everything at the cross. Build your life upon that truth. Let your burdens evaporate. Rejoice that Jesus takes your sins and throws them all away. See your sins from the proper perspective—they are invisible to God.

> The Lord is compassionate and gracious, slow to
> anger, abounding in love ... He does not treat us
> as our sins deserve or repay us according to our
> iniquities ... As far as the east is from the west,

so far has He removed our transgressions from us (Psalm 103:8–12).

Spiritual freedom is the release of personal responsibility for making things right with God. If you still experience guilt, or perhaps live in fear of hell, then it's imperative that you learn to put your faith in Christ, *at all times.* You must believe that righteousness comes *only* through Him (Romans 10:2–4). It's understandable to think that righteousness, and possibly even salvation, depends on you. But the truth is that righteousness is a gift from God, not an achievement for Him.

> Those who receive abundance of grace and the *gift* of righteousness will reign in life through the One, Jesus Christ (Romans 5:17 NKJV).

33

If you're living in the freedom of the Holy Spirit (2 Corinthians 3:17) instead of bogging down in the flesh, then you can be assured that your obedience will improve because of your faith; it will be the result of the power of the Spirit rather than personal effort.

A spirit-filled, freedom-based approach to life seeks Jesus and emphasizes Him in all it does. The result is a joyful obedience to the Lord. A self-based, sin-free approach to life views personal obedience as the ultimate goal. The result is a glorified grind.

We are not called to make life harder than it already is. We are called to give Jesus our burdens in exchange for a supernatural rest (Matthew 11:28–30; Philippians 4:6–7). Once you give all your burdens to Christ—such that you feel completely liberated in His freedom—your obedience will flow from a wellspring of heartfelt gratitude and love; and that's the point where obedience is truly no longer a duty, but a pleasure.

Christians are obedient because we want to be, not because we have to be. It's a desire out of gratitude, not a burden to fulfill. A disposition, not a set of teachings. A way of life, not a list of rules. A matter of the heart, not of outward appearance. A reflection of the Spirit, not a requirement of the flesh. *A faith in Jesus, not in self.*

Though I'm as ordinary as anyone, faith in Christ makes me as extraordinary as anybody who has ever lived on the face of the earth at any time in history, not counting Jesus, of course. But what about Peter? Moses? King David? Mother Teresa? Martin Luther? You can put me on that list. And you belong there too. In fact, you are a perfect being in God's sight—fit for eternal salvation, fit to be a saint.

> This Good News tells us how God makes us right in his sight. This is accomplished *from start to finish* by faith (Romans 1:17 NLT).

By faith, not perfect action, the average Joe is declared righteous and immortal. It's simple faith that transforms us ordinary sinners into everyday saints.

> Let us look only to Jesus, the One who began our faith and who makes it perfect. He suffered death on the cross. But he accepted the shame as if it were nothing because of the joy that God put before him. And now he is sitting at the right side of God's throne (Hebrews 12:2 NCV).

> But because Jesus lives forever, his priesthood lasts forever. Therefore he is able, once and forever, to save those who come to God through him. He lives forever to intercede with God on their behalf. He is the kind of high priest we need because he is holy and blameless, unstained by sin. He has been set apart from sinners and

has been given the highest place of honor in heaven. Unlike those other high priests, he does not need to offer sacrifices every day. They did this for their own sins first and then for the sins of the people. But Jesus did this once for all when he offered himself as the sacrifice for the people's sins (Hebrews 7:24–27 NCV).

We try our best every day, whether in word or deed, spirit or body, at home or work (Colossians 3:23). But as we grow in the Lord, we realize that our best isn't really worth anything. Therefore, we learn to stop nitpicking ourselves apart, because we truly believe that no one can be made righteous by way of effort or performance, but only by faith in Jesus Christ.

Human perfection is not a human accomplishment, but a mind-blowing, terribly fortunate gift. And it is incredibly liberating to accept the gift of perfection in the midst of our ineptitude. Although we don't settle for our spiritual clumsiness, we rejoice deeply that we are declared holy in spite of it!

It is therapeutic to accept that you will never deserve to be called a child of God; but through the blood of Jesus Christ, you are indeed adopted as God's own. You are His perfect offspring. I know it sounds strange, but you have never made a mistake in God's eyes. He loves you so much that He gives *you* the credit for the holiness that Jesus achieved (Romans 4:23–25). And for that reason—no matter what you've done—you can be certain that you will hear these famous words of Christ when He welcomes you home:

Well done, good and faithful servant.

APPENDIX

NEW TESTAMENT SCRIPTURES ON SALVATION

This appendix contains all the passages about salvation from the New Testament. You can expect to find some verses that don't quite make sense to what we think of as salvation, but my goal was to record any passages about eternal life, whatever they may be. I never assumed symbolism, although some may exist, and I didn't account for context; I just kept it as simple as possible. I admit I may have missed a few verses, because I didn't use a concordance or reference software. However, I'm not concerned with any possible omissions, because the main points of the appendix are firmly proven without any layers of translation, symbolism, or explanation:

- There are hundreds of verses about salvation, and we aren't expected to memorize all of them or latch onto the same specific few. Therefore, on the surface, debates about salvation are understandable.
- There's *not one instance* where an exhaustive list for how to be saved is conveniently provided for us in one passage. There's no Master List of Salvation that neatly

summarizes our responsibilities. My assumption is God did that for a reason.

- As this appendix should help us see, eternal life is about Jesus Christ. Jesus Himself is the New Covenant (Hebrews 8:6–7, 13), such that salvation is no longer about us or a code to adhere to. Salvation is not a function of our responsibilities, but His accomplishments. Jesus is our Savior. He has satisfied God's requirements. Our duty is to choose Him.

Throughout the appendix, all Scriptures are from the New Living Translation (NLT) unless indicated otherwise.

Matthew

Matthew 3:11—I baptize with water those who turn from their sins and turn to God. But someone is coming soon who is far greater than I am—so much greater that I am not even worthy to be his slave. He will baptize you with the Holy Spirit and with fire.

Matthew 5:3—God blesses those who realize their need for him, for the Kingdom of Heaven is given to them.

Matthew 5:8—God blesses those whose hearts are pure, for they will see God.

Matthew 5:9—God blesses those who work for peace, for they will be called children of God.

Matthew 5:10—God blesses those who are persecuted because they live for God, for the Kingdom of Heaven is theirs.

Matthew 5:11–12—God blesses you when you are mocked and persecuted and lied about because you are my followers. Be happy about it! Be very glad! For a great reward awaits you in heaven.

Matthew 6:1–2—Don't do your good deeds publicly, to be admired, because then you will lose the reward from your Father in heaven. When you give a gift to someone in need, don't shout about it as the hypocrites do … (They) call attention to their acts of charity! I assure you, they have received all the reward they will ever get.

Matthew 6:5—When you pray, don't be like the hypocrites who love to pray publicly ... where everyone can see them. I assure you: that is all the reward they will ever get.

Matthew 6:14–15—If you forgive those who sin against you, your heavenly Father will forgive you. But if you refuse to forgive others, your Father will not forgive your sins.

Matthew 6:16—And when you fast, don't make it obvious, as the hypocrites do, who try to look pale and disheveled so people will admire them for their fasting. I assure you that is the only reward they will ever get.

Matthew 6:24—You cannot serve both God and money.

Matthew 7:13—You can enter God's Kingdom only through the narrow gate.

Matthew 7:19—Every tree that does not produce good fruit is chopped down and thrown into the fire.

Matthew 7:21–23 (NIV)—Not everyone who says to me, "Lord, Lord," will enter the kingdom of heaven, but only the one who does the will of my Father who is in heaven. Many will say to me on that day, "Lord, Lord, did we not prophesy in your name, and in your name drive out demons and perform many miracles?" Then I will tell them plainly, "I never knew you. Away from me, you evildoers!"

Matthew 9:13—Now go and learn the meaning of this Scripture: "I want you to be merciful; I don't want your sacrifices." For I have come to call sinners, not those who think they are good enough.

Matthew 10:22—And everyone will hate you because of your allegiance to me. But those who endure to the end will be saved.

Matthew 10:32–33—If anyone acknowledges me publicly here on earth, I will openly acknowledge that person before my Father in heaven. But if anyone denies me here on earth, I will deny that person before my Father in heaven.

Matthew 10:37—If you love your father or mother more than you love me, you are not worthy of being mine; or if you love your son or daughter more than me, you are not worthy of being mine.

Matthew 10:38—If you refuse to take up your cross and follow me, you are not worthy of being mine.

Matthew 10:39—If you cling to your life, you will lose it; but if you give it up for me, you will find it.

Matthew 12:36–37 (NIV)—But I tell you that men will have to give account on the day of judgment for every careless word they have spoken. For by your words you will be acquitted, and by your words you will be condemned.

Matthew 12:50—Anyone who does the will of my Father in heaven is my brother and sister and mother.

Matthew 13:43—The godly will shine like the sun in their Father's Kingdom.

Matthew 13:49–50—The angels will come and separate the wicked people from the godly, throwing the wicked into the fire. There will be weeping and gnashing of teeth.

Matthew 15:8–9—These people (Pharisees and teachers of religious law) honor me with their lips, but their hearts are far away. Their worship is a farce, for they replace God's commands with their own man-made teachings.

Matthew 16:24–25—If any of you wants to be my follower, you must put aside your selfish ambition, shoulder your cross, and follow me. If you try to keep your life for yourself, you will lose it. But if you give up your life for me, you will find true life.

Matthew 16:27—For I, the Son of Man, will come in the glory of my Father with his angels and will judge all people according to their deeds.

Matthew 18:3–4—I assure you, unless you turn from your sins and become as little children, you will never get into the Kingdom of Heaven. Therefore, anyone who becomes as humble as this little child is the greatest in the Kingdom of Heaven.

Matthew 19:14—Let the children come to me. Don't stop them! For the Kingdom of Heaven belongs to those such as these.

Matthew 19:16–24—Someone came to Jesus with this question: "Teacher, what good things must I do to have eternal life?" "Why ask me about what is good?" Jesus replied. "Only God is good. But to answer your question, you can receive eternal life if you keep the commandments … Do not murder. Do not commit adultery. Do not steal. Do not testify falsely. Honor your father and mother. Love your neighbor as yourself." "I've obeyed all those commandments," the young man replied. "What else must I do?" Jesus told him, "If you want to be perfect, go and sell all you have and give the money to the poor, and you will have treasure in heaven. Then come, follow me." But when the young man heard this, he went away sadly because he had many possessions. Then Jesus said to his disciples, "I tell you the truth, it is very hard for a rich person to get into the Kingdom of Heaven. I say it again—it is easier for a camel to go through the eye of a needle than for a rich person to enter the Kingdom of God!"

Matthew 19:25–26—The disciples were astounded. "Then who in the world can be saved?" they asked. Jesus looked at them intently and said, "Humanly speaking, it is impossible. But with God everything is possible."

Matthew 19:29—And everyone who has given up houses or brothers or sisters or father or mother or children or property, for my sake, will receive a hundred times as much in return and will have eternal life.

Matthew 21:32—I assure you, corrupt tax collectors and prostitutes will get into the Kingdom of God before you do (the leaders who questioned the authority of Jesus.) For John the Baptist came and showed you the way to life, and you didn't believe him, while tax collectors and prostitutes did. And even when you saw this happening, you refused to turn from your sins and believe him.

Matthew 23:13–15—How terrible it will be for you teachers of religious law and you Pharisees. Hypocrites! For you won't let others enter the Kingdom of Heaven, and you won't go in yourselves. Yes, how terrible it will be for you teachers of religious law and you Pharisees. For you cross land and sea to make one convert, and then you turn him into twice the son of hell as you yourselves are.

Matthew 24:12–13—Sin will be rampant everywhere and the love of many will grow cold. But those who endure to the end will be saved.

Matthew 24:46–51—If the master returns and finds that the servant has done a good job, there will be a reward ... But if the servant is evil and thinks, "My master won't be back for a while," and begins oppressing the other servants, partying, and getting drunk—well, the master will return unannounced and unexpected. He will tear the servant apart and banish him with the hypocrites. In that place there will be weeping and gnashing of teeth.

Matthew 25:29–30—To those who use well what they are given, even more will be given, and they will have an abundance. But from those who are unfaithful, even what little they have will be taken away. Now throw this useless servant into outer darkness, where there will be weeping and gnashing of teeth.

Matthew 25:34–46—Then the King will say to those on the right, "Come, you who are blessed by my Father, inherit the Kingdom prepared for you from the foundation of the world. For I was hungry, and you fed me. I was thirsty, and you gave me a drink. I was a stranger, and you invited me into your home. I was naked, and you gave me clothing. I was sick, and you cared for me. I was in prison, and you visited me." ... Then the

King will turn to those on the left and say, "Away with you, you cursed ones, into the eternal fire prepared for the devil and his demons! ... When you refused to help the least of these my brothers and sisters, you were refusing to help me." And they will go away into eternal punishment, but the righteous will go into eternal life.

Mark

Mark 1:4—(John the Baptist) lived in the wilderness and was preaching that people should be baptized to show that they had turned from their sins and turned to God to be forgiven.

Mark 1:15—The Kingdom of God is near! Turn from your sins and believe this Good News!

Mark 3:28–30—I assure you that any sin can be forgiven, including blasphemy; but anyone who blasphemes against the Holy Spirit will never be forgiven. It is an eternal sin. [Jesus] told them this because they were saying he had an evil spirit.

Mark 3:35—Anyone who does God's will is my brother and sister and mother.

Mark 4:12—They see what I do, but they don't perceive its meaning. They hear my words, but they don't understand. So they will not turn from their sins and be forgiven.

Mark 7:7—These people (Pharisees and teachers of religious law) honor me with their lips, but their hearts are far away. Their worship is a farce, for they replace God's commands with their own man-made teachings.

Mark 8:33–35—Get away from me, Satan! You are seeing things merely from a human point of view, not from God's ... If any of you wants to be my follower ... you must put aside your selfish ambition, shoulder your cross, and follow me. If you try to keep your life for yourself, you will lose it. But if you give up your life for my sake and for the sake of the Good News, you will find true life.

Mark 9:42—If anyone causes one of these little ones who trusts in me to lose faith, it would be better for that person to be thrown into the sea with a large millstone tied around the neck.

Mark 10:14–15—Let the children come to me. Don't stop them! For the Kingdom of God belongs to such as these. I assure you, anyone who doesn't have their kind of faith will never get into the Kingdom of God.

Mark 10:17–23—A man came running up to Jesus, knelt down, and asked, "Good Teacher, what should I do to get eternal life?" "Why do you call me good?" Jesus asked. "Only God is truly good. But as for your question, you know the commandments: 'Do not murder. Do not commit adultery. Do not steal. Do not testify falsely. Do not cheat. Honor your father and mother.'" "Teacher," the man replied, "I've obeyed all these commandments since I was a child." Jesus felt genuine love for the man as He looked at him. "You lack only one thing," He told him. "Go and sell all you have and give the money to the poor, and you will have treasure in heaven. Then come, follow me." ... How hard it is for rich people to get into the Kingdom of God!

Mark 10:26–27—Who in the world can be saved? … Humanly speaking, it is impossible. But not with God. Everything is possible with God.

Mark 10:29–30—I assure you that everyone who has given up house or brothers or sisters or mother of father or children or property, for my sake and for the Good News, will receive now in return, a hundred times over, houses, brothers, sisters, mothers, children, and property—with persecutions. And in the world to come they will have eternal life.

Mark 11:25—But when you are praying, first forgive anyone you are holding a grudge against, so that your Father in heaven will forgive your sins, too.

Mark 12:29–31—The most important commandment is this: Hear, O Israel! The Lord our God is the one and only Lord. And you must love the Lord your God with all your heart, all your soul, all your mind, and all your strength. The second is equally important: Love your neighbor as yourself. No other commandment is greater than these.

Mark 13:13—Everyone will hate you because of your allegiance to me. But those who endure to the end will be saved.

Mark 16:16—Anyone who believes and is baptized will be saved. But anyone who refuses to believe will be condemned.

Luke

Luke 1:77—People … find salvation through forgiveness of their sins.

Luke 2:34—This child (Jesus) will be rejected by many ... and it will be their undoing. But he will be the greatest joy to many others.

Luke 3:3—John went from place to place on both sides of the Jordan River, preaching that people should be baptized to show that they had turned from their sins and turned to God to be forgiven.

Luke 3:7–9—Who warned you to flee God's judgment? Prove by the way you live that you have really turned from your sins and turned to God ... Yes, every tree that does not produce good fruit will be chopped down and thrown into the fire.

Luke 5:20—Seeing their faith, Jesus said to the man, "Son, your sins are forgiven."

Luke 5:32—I have come to call sinners to turn from their sins, not to spend my time with those who think they are already good enough.

Luke 6:35–36—Love your enemies! Do good to them! Lend to them! And don't be concerned that they might not repay. Then your reward in heaven will be very great, and you will truly be acting as children of the Most High, for he is kind to the unthankful and to those who are wicked. You must be compassionate just as your Father is compassionate.

Luke 7:47–50—I tell you, her sins—and they are many—have been forgiven, so she has shown me much love. But a person who is forgiven little shows only little love. Then Jesus said to the woman, "Your sins are forgiven ... Your faith has saved you; go in peace."

Luke 8:21—My mother and my brothers are all those who hear the message of God and obey it.

Luke 9:24–25—If any of you wants to be my follower, you must put aside your selfish ambition, shoulder your cross daily, and follow me. If you try to keep your life for yourself, you will lose it. But if you give up your life for me, you will find true life.

Luke 9:62—Anyone who puts a hand to the plow and then looks back is not fit for the Kingdom of God.

Luke 10:16—Then he said to the disciples, "Anyone who accepts your message is also accepting me. And anyone who rejects you is rejecting me. And anyone who rejects me is rejecting God who sent me."

Luke 10:21—Then Jesus was filled with the Holy Spirit and said, "O Father, Lord of heaven and earth, thank you for hiding the truth from those who think themselves so wise and clever, and for revealing it to the childlike. Yes, Father, it pleased you to do it this way."

Luke 10:27–28—You must love the Lord your God with all your heart, all your soul, all your strength, and all your mind. And, love your neighbor as yourself ... Do this and you will live.

Luke 11:28—Blessed are all who hear the word of God and put it into practice.

Luke 11:52—How terrible it will be for you experts in religious law! For you hide the key to knowledge from the people. You don't enter the Kingdom yourselves, and you prevent others from entering.

Luke 12:8–10—If anyone acknowledges me publicly here on earth, I, the Son of Man, will openly acknowledge that person in the presence of God's angels. But if anyone denies me here on earth, I will deny that person before God's angels. Yet those who speak against the Son of Man may be forgiven, but anyone who speaks blasphemies against the Holy Spirit will never be forgiven.

Luke 12:45–46—If the servant thinks, "My master won't be back for awhile," and begins oppressing the other servants, partying, and getting drunk—well, the master will return unannounced and unexpected. He will tear the servant apart and banish him with the unfaithful.

Luke 13:3, 5—You will also perish unless you turn from your evil ways and turn to God ... I will tell you again that unless you repent, you will also perish.

Luke 14:14—At the resurrection of the godly, God will reward you for inviting those who could not repay you.

Luke 14:26–27, 33—If you want to be my follower you must love me more than your own father and mother, wife and children, brothers and sisters—yes, more than your own life. Otherwise, you cannot be my disciple. And you cannot be my disciple if you do not carry your own cross and follow me ... So no one can become my disciple without giving up everything else for me.

Luke 16:9–13—I tell you, use your worldly resources to benefit others and make friends. In this way, your generosity stores up a reward for you in heaven ... And if you are untrustworthy about worldly wealth, who will trust you with the true riches of heaven? ... No one can serve two masters ... You cannot serve both God and money.

Luke 16:25—(Rich man who overlooked the hungry and poor), remember that during your lifetime you had everything you wanted, and Lazarus (a diseased beggar whom the rich man did not help) had nothing. So now he is here being comforted, and you are in anguish.

Luke 17:32–33—Remember what happened to Lot's wife! Whoever clings to this life will lose it, and whoever loses this life will save it.

Luke 18:8—But when I, the Son of Man, return, how many will I find who have faith?

Luke 18:11–14—The proud Pharisee stood by himself and prayed this prayer: "I thank you, God, that I am not a sinner like everyone else, especially like that tax collector over there! For I never cheat, I don't sin, I don't commit adultery, I fast twice a week, and I give you a tenth of my income." But the tax collector stood at a distance and dared not even lift his eyes to heaven as he prayed. Instead, he beat his chest in sorrow, saying, "O God, be merciful to me, for I am a sinner." I tell you, this sinner, not the Pharisee, returned home justified before God.

Luke 18:16–17—Let the children come to me. Don't stop them! For the Kingdom of God belongs to such as these. I assure you, anyone who doesn't have their kind of faith will never get into the Kingdom of God.

Luke 18:18–25—"Good teacher, what should I do to get eternal life?" … "you know the commandments: 'Do not commit adultery. Do not murder. Do not steal. Do not testify falsely. Honor your father and mother.'" The man replied, "I've obeyed all these commandments since I was a child." "There is still one thing you lack," Jesus said. "Sell all you have and give the money to the poor, and you will have treasure in heaven. Then come, follow me." But when the man heard this, he became sad because he was very rich. Jesus watched him go and then said to his disciples, "How hard it is for rich people to get into the Kingdom of God! It is easier for a camel to go through the eye of a needle than for a rich person to enter the Kingdom of God!"

Luke 18:26–27—Who in the world can be saved? … What is impossible from a human perspective is possible with God.

Luke 18:29–30—Everyone who has given up house or wife or brothers or parents or children, for the sake of the Kingdom of God, will be repaid many times over in this life, as well as receiving eternal life in the world to come.

Luke 19:8–10—Zacchaeus stood there and said to the Lord, "I will give half my wealth to the poor, Lord, and if I have overcharged people on their taxes, I will give them back four times as much!" Jesus responded, "Salvation has come to this home today, for this man has shown himself to be a son of Abraham. And I, the Son of Man have come to seek and save those like him who are lost."

Luke 21:19—By standing firm, you will win your souls.

Luke 21:34, 36—Watch out! Don't let me find you living in careless ease and drunkenness, and filled with the worries of this life ... Pray that ... you may escape these horrors and stand before the Son of Man.

Luke 23:40–43—But the other criminal protested, "Don't you fear God even when you are dying? We deserve to die for our evil deeds, but this man hasn't done anything wrong." Then he said, "Jesus, remember me when you come into your Kingdom." And Jesus replied, "I assure you, today you will be with me in paradise."

Luke 24:47—Take this message of repentance to all the nations, beginning in Jerusalem: "There is forgiveness of sins for all who turn to me."

John

John 1:12—But to all who believed him and accepted him, he gave the right to become children of God.

John 3:3–8—Jesus replied, "I assure you, unless you are born again, you can never see the Kingdom of God ... The truth is, no one can enter the Kingdom of God without being born of water and the Spirit. Humans can reproduce only human life, but the Holy Spirit gives new life from heaven. So don't be surprised at my statement that you must be born again. Just as you can hear the wind but can't tell where it comes from or where it is going, so you can't explain how people are born of the Spirit."

John 3:14–18—I, the Son of Man, must be lifted up on a pole, so that everyone who believes in me will have eternal life. For God so loved the world that he gave his only Son, so that everyone who believes in him will not perish but have eternal life. God did not send his Son into the world to condemn it, but to save it. There is no judgment awaiting those who trust him. But those who do not trust him have already been judged for not believing in the only Son of God.

John 3:36—And all who believe in God's Son have eternal life. Those who don't obey the Son will never experience eternal life, but the wrath of God remains upon them.

John 4:10, 14—If you only knew the gift God has for you and who I am, you would ask me, and I would give you living water … But the water I give them takes away thirst altogether. It becomes a perpetual spring within them, giving them eternal life.

John 5:24–25—I assure you, those who listen to my message and believe in God who sent me have eternal life. They will never be condemned for their sins, but they have already passed from death into life … And those who listen will live.

John 5:29—Those who have done good will rise to eternal life and those who have continued in evil will rise to judgment.

John 5:34—But the best testimony about me is not from a man, though I have reminded you about John's (the Baptist) testimony so you might be saved.

John 5:38–42—And you do not have (God's) message in your hearts, because you do not believe me—the one he sent to you.

You search the Scriptures because you believe they give you eternal life. But the Scriptures point to me! Yet you refuse to come to me so that I can give you this eternal life. Your approval or disapproval means nothing to me, because I know you don't have God's love within you.

John 6:27–29—But you shouldn't be so concerned about perishable things like food. Spend your energy seeking the eternal life that I, the Son of Man, can give you. For God the Father has sent me for that very purpose. They replied, "What does God want us to do?" Jesus told them, "This is what God wants you to do: Believe in the one he has sent."

John 6:33—The true bread of God is the one who comes down from heaven and gives life to the world.

John 6:35—I am the bread of life. No one who comes to me will ever be hungry again. Those who believe in me will never thirst.

John 6:39–40—And this is the will of God, that I should not lose even one of all those he has given me, but that I should raise them to eternal life at the last day. For it is my Father's will that all who see his Son and believe in him should have eternal life—that I should raise them at the last day.

John 6:47—I assure you, anyone who believes in me already has eternal life.

John 6:50–58—However, the bread from heaven gives eternal life to everyone who eats it. I am the living bread that came out of heaven. Anyone who eats this bread will live forever; this bread is my flesh, offered so the world may live ... I assure you, unless you eat the flesh of the Son of Man and drink his blood, you cannot have eternal life within you. But those who eat my flesh and drink my blood have eternal life, and I will raise them at the last day … I am the true bread from heaven. Anyone who eats this bread will live forever.

John 6:63—It is the Spirit who gives eternal life. Human effort accomplishes nothing. And the very words I have spoken to you are spirit and life.

John 6:68–69—Simon Peter replied, "Lord, to whom would we go? You alone have the words that give eternal life. We believe them, and we know you are the Holy One of God."

John 8:12—Jesus said to the people, "I am the light of the world. If you follow me, you won't be stumbling through the darkness, because you will have the light that leads to life.

John 8:24—Unless you believe who I say I am, you will die in your sins.

John 8:51—I assure you, anyone who obeys my teaching will never die.

John 10:9—Yes, I am the gate. Those who come in through me will be saved. Wherever they go, they will find green pastures.

John 10:27–28—My sheep recognize my voice; I know them, and they follow me. I give them eternal life, and they will never perish.

John 11:25–26—I am the resurrection and the life. Those who believe in me, even though they die like everyone else, will live again. They are given eternal life for believing in me and will never perish. Do you believe this, Martha?

John 11:40—Jesus responded, "Didn't I tell you that you will see God's glory if you believe?"

John 12:25—Those who love their life in this world will lose it. Those who despise their life in this world will keep it for eternal life.

John 12:36—Believe in the light while there is still time; then you will become children of the light.

John 12:44–50—If you trust me, you are really trusting God … I have come as a light to shine in this dark world, so that all who put their trust in me will no longer remain in the darkness … I have come to save the world and not to judge it. But all who reject me and my message will be judged at the day of judgment by the truth I have spoken. I don't speak on my own authority. The Father … gave me his instructions … his instructions lead to eternal life.

John 13:34–35—So now I am giving you a new commandment: Love each other. Just as I have loved you, you should love each other. Your love for one another will prove to the world that you are my disciples.

John 14:6—I am the way, the truth, and the life. No one can come to the Father except through me.

John 15:4, 6—Remain in me, and I will remain in you … Anyone who parts from me is thrown away like a useless branch.

John 17:3—And this is the way to have eternal life—to know you, the only true God, and Jesus Christ, the one you sent to earth.

John 21:31—Believe that Jesus is the Messiah, the Son of God, and by believing in him you will have life.

Acts

Acts 2:21—And anyone who calls on the name of the Lord will be saved.

Acts 2:38–39—Each of you must turn from your sins and turn to God, and be baptized in the name of Jesus Christ for the forgiveness of your sins. Then you will receive the gift of the Holy Spirit. This promise is to you and to your children, and even to the Gentiles—all who have been called by the Lord our God.

Acts 2:41—Those who believed what Peter said were baptized and added to the church.

Acts 3:19—Turn from your sins and turn to God, so you can be cleansed of your sins.

Acts 4:12—There is salvation in no one else (but Jesus)! There is no other name in all of heaven for people to call on to save them.

Acts 8:12 (NIV)—But when they believed Philip as he proclaimed the good news of the kingdom of God and the name of Jesus Christ, they were baptized, both men and women.

Acts 8:35–38 (NIV)—Then Philip … told him the good news about Jesus. As they traveled along the road, they came to some water and the eunuch said, "Look, here is water. What can stand in the way of my being baptized?" [Some manuscripts include here: *Philip said, "If you believe with all your heart, you may." The eunuch answered, "I believe that Jesus Christ is the Son of God."*] And he gave orders to stop the chariot ... and Philip baptized him.

Acts 9:17—So Ananias went and found Saul. He laid his hands on him and said, "Brother Saul, the Lord Jesus, who appeared to you on the road, has sent me so that you many get your sight back and be filled with the Holy Spirit." Instantly something like scales fell from Saul's eyes, and he regained his sight. Then he got up and was baptized.

Acts 10:34–36—I see very clearly that God doesn't show partiality. In every nation he accepts those who fear him and do what is right ... There is peace with God through Jesus Christ, who is Lord of all.

Acts 10:43—(Jesus) is the one all the prophets testified about, saying that everyone who believes in him will have their sins forgiven through his name.

Acts 10:46–48—Then Peter asked, "Can anyone object to their being baptized, now that they have received the Holy Spirit just as we did?" So he gave orders for them to be baptized in the name of Jesus Christ.

Acts 11:14, 18 (NIV)—He will bring you a message through which you and all your household will be saved. When they heard this, they had no further objections and praised God, saying, "So then, even to Gentiles God has granted repentance that leads to life."

Acts 13:38–39—In this man Jesus there is forgiveness for your sins. Everyone who believes in him is freed from all guilt and declared right with God—something the Jewish law could never do.

Acts 13:46–48—It was necessary that this Good News be given first to you Jews. But since you have rejected it and judged yourselves unworthy of eternal life, we will offer it to Gentiles. For this is as the Lord commanded us when he said, "I have made you a light to the Gentiles, to bring salvation to the farthest corners of the earth." When the Gentiles heard this, they were very glad and thanked the Lord for his message; and all who were appointed to eternal life became believers.

Acts 14:22—They strengthened the believers. They encouraged them to continue in the faith, reminding them that they must enter into the Kingdom of God through many tribulations.

Acts 15:8–11—God, who knows people's hearts, confirmed that he accepts Gentiles by giving them the Holy Spirit, just as he gave him to us. He made no distinction between us and them, for he also cleansed their hearts through faith. Why are you now questioning God's way by burdening the Gentile believers with a yoke that neither we nor our ancestors were able to bear? We believe that we are all saved the same way, by the special favor of the Lord Jesus.

Acts 15:19–20; 28–29—We should stop troubling the Gentiles who turn to God, except that we should write ... "For it seemed good to the Holy Spirit and to us to lay no greater burden on you except these requirements: You must abstain from eating food offered to idols, from consuming blood or eating the meat of strangled animals, and from sexual immorality. If you do this, you will do well."

Acts 16:14–15—(Lydia) was a worshiper of God. As she listened to us, the Lord opened her heart, and she accepted what Paul was saying. She was baptized.

Acts 16:30–34—(The jailer) brought (Paul and Silas) and asked, "Sirs, what must I do to be saved?" They replied, "Believe on the Lord Jesus and you will be saved, along with your entire household." Then they shared the word of the Lord with him and all who lived in his household ... He and everyone in his household were immediately baptized ... (They) rejoiced because they all believed in God.

Acts 18:8—Crispus, the leader of the Synagogue, and all his household believed in the Lord. Many others in Corinth also became believers and were baptized.

Acts 19:3–5—"What baptism did you experience?" he asked. And they replied, "The baptism of John." Paul said, "John's baptism was to demonstrate a desire to turn from sin and turn to God. John himself told the people to believe in Jesus..." As soon as they heard this, they were baptized in the name of the Lord Jesus.

Acts 20:21—I have had one message for Jews and Gentiles alike—the necessity of turning from sin and turning to God, and of faith in our Lord Jesus.

Acts 22:16—Why delay? Get up and be baptized, and have your sins washed away, calling on the name of the Lord.

Acts 26:18—Open their eyes so they may turn from darkness to light and from the power of Satan to God. Then they will receive forgiveness for their sins and be given a place among God's people, who are set apart by faith in me.

Acts 26:20—All must turn from their sins and turn to God, and prove they have changed by the good things they do.

Romans

Romans 1:16–17—I am not ashamed of this Good News about Christ. It is the power of God at work, saving everyone who believes … This Good News tells us how God makes us right in his sight. This is accomplished from start to finish by faith. As the Scriptures say, "The righteous will live by faith."

Romans 2:7—He will give eternal life to those who persist in doing what is good, seeking after the glory and honor and immortality that God offers.

Romans 3:21–22—God has shown us a different way of being right in his sight—not by obeying the law … We are made right in God's sight when we trust in Jesus Christ to take away our sins. And we all can be saved in this same way, no matter who we are or what we have done.

Romans 3:24–25—God in his gracious kindness declares us not guilty. He has done this through Christ Jesus, who has freed us by taking away our sins. For God sent Jesus to take the punishment for our sins and to satisfy God's anger against us. We are made right with God when we believe that Jesus shed his blood, sacrificing his life for us.

Romans 3:26—(God) declares sinners to be right in his sight because they believe in Jesus.

Romans 3:27–28—Our acquittal is not based on our good deeds. It is based on our faith. So we are made right with God through faith and not by obeying the law.

Romans 3:30—There is only one God, and there is only one way of being accepted by him. He makes people right with himself only by faith.

Romans 4:3, 22—Abraham believed God, so God declared him to be righteous.

Romans 4:5—People are declared righteous because of their faith not because of their work.

Romans 4:10–11—Was (Abraham) declared righteous only after he had been circumcised, or was it before he was circumcised? The answer is that God accepted him first, and then he was circumcised later! The circumcision ceremony was a sign that Abraham already had faith and that God had already accepted him and declared him to be righteous—even before he was circumcised. So Abraham is the spiritual father of those who have faith … They are made right with God by faith.

Romans 4:13–14—It is clear, then, that God's promise … was not based on obedience to God's law, but on the new relationship with God that comes by faith. So if you claim that God's promise is for those who obey God's law and think they are "good enough" in God's sight, then you are saying that faith is useless.

Romans 4:16—God's promise is given to us as a free gift. And we are certain to receive it, whether or not we follow Jewish customs, if we have faith.

Romans 4:24 (NIV)—God will credit righteousness for us who believe in him who raised Jesus our Lord from the dead.

Romans 5:1–2—Therefore, since we have been made right in God's sight by faith, we have peace with God because of what Jesus Christ our Lord has done for us. Because of our faith, Christ has brought us into this place.

Romans 5:9–11—And since we have been made right in God's sight by the blood of Christ, he will certainly save us from God's judgment ... We will certainly be delivered from eternal punishment by his life. We can rejoice in our wonderful new relationship with God—all because of what our Lord Jesus Christ has done for us in making us friends of God.

Romans 5:15–19—Jesus Christ brought forgiveness to many through God's bountiful gift ... We have the free gift of being accepted by God, even though we are guilty of many sins ... All who receive God's wonderful, gracious gift of righteousness will live in triumph over sin and death through this one man, Jesus Christ ... Christ's one act of righteousness makes all people right in God's sight and gives them life ... But because one other person obeyed God, many people will be made right in God's sight.

Romans 5:21 (NCV)—God gave people more of his grace so that grace could rule by making people right with him. And this brings life forever through Jesus Christ our Lord.

Romans 6:3–8—When we became Christians and were baptized to become one with Christ Jesus, we died with him. For we died and were buried with Christ by baptism. And just as Christ was raised from the dead by the glorious power of the Father, now we also may live new lives. Since we have been united with him in his death, we will also be raised as he was. Our old sinful selves were crucified with Christ so that sin might lose its power in our lives. We are no longer slaves to sin. For when we died with Christ we were set free from the power of sin. And since we died with Christ, we know we will also share his new life.

Romans 6:14—Sin is no longer your master, for you are no longer subject to the law, which enslaves you to sin. Instead, you are free by God's grace.

Romans 6:22–23—Now you are free from the power of sin and have become slaves of God. Now you do those things that lead to holiness and result in eternal life. For the wages of sin is death, but the free gift of God is eternal life through Christ Jesus our Lord.

Romans 8:3–4; 9–11—The law of Moses could not save us, because of our sinful nature. But God put into effect a different plan to save us. He sent his own Son in a human body like ours … God destroyed sin's control over us by giving his Son as a sacrifice for our sins. He did this so that the requirement of the law would be fully accomplished for us who no longer follow our sinful nature but instead follow the Spirit … You are controlled by the Spirit if you have the Spirit of God living in you. (And remember that those who do not have the Spirit of Christ living in them are not Christians at all.) Since Christ lives within you … your spirit is alive because you have been made right with God.

Romans 8:15–16—You should not be like cowering, fearful slaves. You should behave instead like God's very own children, adopted into his family—calling Him, "Father, dear Father." For his Holy Spirit speaks to us deep in our hearts and tells us that we are God's children.

Romans 8:34—Who then will condemn us? Will Christ Jesus? No, for he is the one who died for us and was raised to life for us and is sitting at the place of highest honor next to God, pleading for us.

Romans 9:30–33—The Gentiles have been made right with God by faith … But the Jews, who tried so hard to get right with God by keeping the law, never succeeded. Why not? Because they were trying to get right with God by keeping the law and being good instead of by depending on faith … Anyone who believes in him will not be disappointed.

Romans 10:2–4—I know what enthusiasm they have for God, but it is misdirected zeal. For they don't understand God's way of making people right with himself. Instead, they are clinging to their own way of getting right with God by trying to keep the law. They won't go along with God's way. For Christ has accomplished the whole purpose of the law. All who believe in him are made right with God.

Romans 10:5–14—Moses wrote that the law's way of making a person right with God requires obedience to all of its commands. But … salvation that comes from trusting Christ—which is the message we preach—is already within easy reach … For if you confess with your mouth that Jesus is Lord and believe in your heart that God raised him from the dead, you will be saved. For it is by believing in your heart that you are made right with God, and it is by confessing with your mouth that you are saved ... Jew and Gentile are the same in this respect. They all have the same Lord, who generously gives his riches to all who ask for them. For "Anyone who calls on the name of the Lord will be saved." But how can they call on him to save them unless they believe in him?

Romans 11:5–6—Not all the Jews have turned away from God. A few are being saved as a result of God's kindness ... And if they are saved by God's kindness, then it is not by their good works. For in that case, God's wonderful kindness would not be what it really is—free and undeserved.

Romans 11:22—Notice how God is both kind and severe. He is severe to those who disobeyed, but kind to you as you continue to trust in his kindness. But if you stop trusting, you also will be cut off.

Romans 13:8–10—If you love your neighbor, you will fulfill all the requirements of God's law. For the commandments ... are all summed up in this one command: "Love your neighbor as yourself." Love does no wrong to anyone, so love satisfies all of God's requirements.

First Corinthians

1 Corinthians 1:2—You who have been called by God to be his own holy people. He made you holy by means of Christ Jesus, just as he did all Christians everywhere—whoever calls upon the name of Jesus Christ, our Lord and theirs.

1 Corinthians 1:30—God alone made it possible for you to be in Christ Jesus. For our benefit God made Christ to be wisdom itself. He is the one who made us acceptable to God. He made us pure and holy, and he gave himself to purchase our freedom.

1 Corinthians 5:5—Cast this man out of the church and into Satan's hands, so that his sinful nature will be destroyed and he himself will be saved when the Lord returns.

1 Corinthians 6:9–13—Don't you know that those who do wrong will have no share in the Kingdom of God? Don't fool yourselves. Those who indulge in sexual sin, who are idol worshipers, adulterers, male prostitutes, homosexuals, thieves, greedy people, drunkards, abusers, and swindlers—none of these will have a share in the Kingdom of God. There was a time when some of you were just like that, but now your sins have been washed away, and you have been made right with God because of what the Lord Jesus Christ and the Spirit of our God have done for you. You may say, "I am allowed to do anything." But I reply, "Not everything is good for you." And even though "I am allowed to do anything," I must not become a slave to anything ... Our bodies were not made for sexual immorality.

1 Corinthians 8:3—The person who loves God is the one God knows and cares for.

1 Corinthians 8:6—There is only one Lord, Jesus Christ, through whom God made everything and through whom we have been given life.

1 Corinthians 12:13—We have all been baptized into Christ's body by one Spirit, and we have all received the same Spirit. Yes, the body has many different parts, not just one part.

1 Corinthians 15:1–3—Now let me remind you of the Good News I preached to you before. You welcomed it then and still do now, for your faith is built on this wonderful message. And it is this Good News that saves you if you firmly believe it—unless, of course, you believed something that was never true in the first place. I passed on to you what was most important and what had also been passed on to me—that Christ died for our sins.

Second Corinthians

2 Corinthians 1:22—He has identified us as his own by placing the Holy Spirit in our hearts.

2 Corinthians 3:6—This is a new covenant, not of written laws, but of the Spirit. The old way ends in death; in the new way, the Holy Spirit gives life.

2 Corinthians 3:14—A veil covers their minds so they cannot understand the truth. And this veil can be removed only by believing in Christ.

2 Corinthians 3:16–18—Whenever anyone turns to the Lord, then the veil is taken away … Wherever the Spirit of the Lord is, he gives freedom … As the Spirit of the Lord works within us, we become more and more like him.

2 Corinthians 5:4–5—We want to slip into our new bodies so that these dying bodies will be swallowed up by everlasting life. God himself has prepared us for this, and as a guarantee he has given us his Holy Spirit.

2 Corinthians 5:10—We must all stand before Christ to be judged. We will each receive whatever we deserve for the good or evil we have done in our bodies.

2 Corinthians 5:14–15—Christ died for everyone ... He died for everyone so that those who receive his new life will no longer live to please themselves. Instead, they will live to please Christ.

2 Corinthians 5:17—Those who become Christians become new persons. They are not the same anymore, for the old life is gone. A new life has begun!

2 Corinthians 5:19, 21; 6:1–2—God ... (is) no longer counting people's sins against them. This is the wonderful message he has given us to tell others ... God made Christ, who never sinned, to be the offering for our sin, so that we could be made right with God through Christ ... We beg you not to reject this marvelous message of God's great kindness. For God says, "At just the right time, I heard you. On the day of salvation, I helped you." Indeed, God is ready to help you right now. Today is the day of salvation.

2 Corinthians 7:10—God can use sorrow in our lives to help us turn away from sin and seek salvation. We will never regret that kind of sorrow. But sorrow without repentance is the kind that results in death.

Galatians

Galatians 2:16—Christians know that we become right with God, not by doing what the law commands, but by faith in Jesus Christ ... No one will ever be saved by obeying the law.

Galatians 2:18–21—I make myself guilty if I rebuild the old system I already tore down. For when I tried to keep the law, I realized I could never earn God's approval. So I died to the law so that I might live for God. I have been crucified with Christ. I myself no longer live, but Christ lives in me. So I live my life in this earthly body by trusting in the Son of God, who loved me and gave himself for me. I am not one of those who treats the grace of God as meaningless. For if we could be saved by keeping the law, then there was no need for Christ to die.

Galatians 3:2–3—Let me ask you this one question: Did you receive the Holy Spirit by keeping the law? Of course not, The Holy Spirit came upon you only after you believed the message you heard about Christ. Have you lost your senses? After starting Christian lives in the Spirit, why are you now trying to become perfect by your own human effort?

Galatians 3:5—Does God give you the Holy Spirit … because you obey the law of Moses? Of course not! It is because you believe the message you heard about Christ.

Galatians 3:7–14—The real children of Abraham, then, are all those who put their faith in God … (God accepts) the Gentiles, too, on the basis of their faith … All who put their faith in Christ share the same blessing Abraham received because of his faith. But those who depend on the law to make them right with God are under his curse … No one can ever be made right with God by trying to keep the law … It is through faith that a righteous person has life. How different from this way of faith is the way of law … But Christ rescued us from the curse pronounced by the law … We Christians receive the Holy Spirit through faith.

Galatians 3:22–26—We are all prisoners of sin, so the only way to receive God's promise is to believe in Jesus Christ. Until faith in Christ was shown to us as the way of becoming right with God, we were guarded by the law … The law was our guardian and teacher until Christ came. So now, through faith in Christ, we are made right with God … So you are all children of God through faith in Christ Jesus.

Galatians 4:31—We are not … obligated to the law. We are … acceptable to God because of our faith.

Galatians 5:4–6—If you are trying to make yourself right with God by keeping the law, you have been cut off from Christ! You have fallen away from God's grace. But we who live by the Spirit eagerly wait to receive everything promised to us who are right with God through faith. For when we place our faith in Christ Jesus, it makes no difference if we are circumcised … What is important is faith expressing itself in love.

Galatians 5:11—The fact that I am still being persecuted proves that I am still preaching salvation through the cross of Christ alone.

Galatians 5:19–21—When you follow the desires of your sinful nature … hostility, quarreling, jealousy, outbursts of anger, selfish ambition, divisions, the feeling that everyone is wrong except those in your own little group, envy, drunkenness, wild parties … anyone living that sort of life will not inherit the Kingdom of God.

Galatians 6:8–10—Those who live to please the Spirit will harvest everlasting life from the Spirit. So don't get tired of doing what is good. Don't get discouraged and give up, for we will reap a harvest of blessing at the appropriate time ... Do good to everyone, especially to our Christian brothers and sisters.

Galatians 6:12—Those who are trying to force you to be circumcised are doing it for just one reason. They don't want to be persecuted for teaching that the cross of Christ alone can save.

Galatians 6:15–16—It doesn't make any difference now whether we have been circumcised or not. What counts is whether we really have been changed into new and different people. May God's mercy and peace be upon all those who live by this principle. They are the new people of God.

Ephesians

Ephesians 1:13—God saves you. And when you believed in Christ, he identified you as his own by giving you the Holy Spirit.

Ephesians 2:5 (NIV)—It is by grace you have been saved.

Ephesians 2:8–9 (NIV)—For it is by grace you have been saved, through faith—and this is not from yourselves, it is the gift of God—not by works, so that no one can boast.

Ephesians 2:13—Though you were once far away from God, now you have been brought near to him because of the blood of Christ.

Ephesians 2:18—Now all of us ... may come to the Father through the same Holy Spirit because of what Christ has done for us.

Ephesians 2:21—We who believe are carefully joined together, becoming a holy temple for the Lord.

Ephesians 3:12—Because of Christ and our faith in him, we can now come fearlessly into God's presence, assured of his glad welcome.

Ephesians 4:30—Do not bring sorrow to God's Holy Spirit by the way you live. Remember, he is the one who has identified you as his own, guaranteeing that you will be saved on the day of redemption.

Ephesians 5:5–9—You can be sure that no immoral, impure, or greedy person will inherit the Kingdom of Christ and of God. For a greedy person is really an idolater who worships things of this world. Don't be fooled by those who try to excuse these sins ... Now you are full of light from the Lord, and your behavior should show it! For this light within you produces only what is good and right and true.

Ephesians 6:24—May God's grace be upon all who love our Lord Jesus Christ with an undying love.

Philippians

Philippians 1:1—This letter ... is written to all of God's people in Philippi, who believe in Christ Jesus.

Philippians 1:28—Don't be intimidated by your enemies. This will be a sign to them that they are going to be destroyed, but that you are going to be saved, even by God himself.

Philippians 3:2–3—Watch out for those dogs, those wicked men … who say you must be circumcised to be saved. We who worship God in the Spirit are the only ones who are truly circumcised. We put no confidence in human effort. Instead we boast about what Christ Jesus has done for us.

Philippians 3:6–9—I obeyed the Jewish law so carefully that I was never accused of any fault. I once thought all these things were so very important, but now I consider them worthless because of what Christ has done. Yes, everything else is worthless when compared with the priceless gain of knowing Christ Jesus my Lord. I have discarded everything else, counting it all as garbage, so that I may have Christ and become one with him. I no longer count on my own goodness or my ability to obey God's law, but I trust Christ to save me. For God's way of making us right with himself depends on faith.

Philippians 3:18–19—There are many whose conduct shows they are really enemies of the cross of Christ. Their future is eternal destruction. Their god is their appetite, they brag about shameful things, and all they think about is this life here on earth.

Colossians

Colossians 1:22–23—His death on the cross … has brought you into the very presence of God, and you are holy and blameless as you stand before him without a single fault. But you must continue to believe this truth and stand in it firmly.

Colossians 1:27—Christ lives in you, and this is your assurance that you will share in his glory.

Colossians 2:2–4—Be encouraged and knit together by strong ties of love ... Have complete understanding of God's secret plan, which is Christ himself. In him lie hidden all the treasures of wisdom and knowledge. I am telling you this so that no one will be able to deceive you with persuasive arguments.

Colossians 2:10–14—You are complete through your union with Christ ... When you came to Christ, you were "circumcised", but not by a physical procedure. It was a spiritual procedure—the cutting away of your sinful nature. For you were buried with Christ when you were baptized. And with him you were raised to a new life because you trusted the mighty power of God ... You were dead because of your sins ... Then God made you alive with Christ. He forgave all our sins. He canceled the record that contained the charges against us. He took it and destroyed it by nailing it to Christ's cross.

First Thessalonians

1 Thessalonians 1:5—The Holy Spirit gave you full assurance that what we said was true. And you know that the way we lived among you was further proof of the truth of our message.

1 Thessalonians 2:12–13—Live your lives in a way that God would consider worthy. For he called you into his Kingdom to share his glory ... This word continues to work in you who believe.

1 Thessalonians 3:12–13—And may the Lord make your love grow and overflow to each other and to everyone else, just as our love overflows toward you. As a result, Christ will make your hearts strong, blameless, and holy when you stand before God our Father on that day when our Lord Jesus comes.

Second Thessalonians

2 Thessalonians 1:10—You will be among those praising him on that day, for you believed what we testified about him.

2 Thessalonians 2:10—He will use every kind of wicked deception to fool those who are on their way to destruction because they refuse to believe the truth that would save them.

2 Thessalonians 2:13—God chose you ... to experience salvation, a salvation that came through the Spirit who makes you holy and by your belief in the truth.

First Timothy

1 Timothy 2:3–6—God our Savior wants everyone to be saved and to understand the truth ... Christ Jesus gave his life to purchase freedom for everyone. This is the message God gave to the world.

1 Timothy 2:15—Women will be saved through childbearing (as a gender) and by continuing to live in faith, love, holiness, and modesty (as an individual).

1 Timothy 4:10—Believe the truth, for our hope is in the living God, who is the Savior of all people, and particularly of those who believe.

1 Timothy 4:16—Keep a close watch on yourself and on your teaching. Stay true to what is right, and God will save you and those who hear you.

Second Timothy

2 Timothy 1:1—Tell others about the life he has promised through faith in Christ Jesus.

2 Timothy 1:9–10; 2:8—It is God who saved us and chose us to live a holy life. He did this not because we deserved it, but because that was his plan ... to show his love and kindness to us through Christ Jesus ... who broke the power of death and showed us the way to everlasting life through the Good News ... Never forget that Jesus Christ ... was raised from the dead. This is the Good News I preach.

2 Timothy 2:15—Work hard so God can approve you.

2 Timothy 2:19—Those who claim they belong to the Lord must turn away from all wickedness.

2 Timothy 3:15—You have been taught the holy Scriptures from childhood, and they have given you the wisdom to receive the salvation that comes by trusting in Christ Jesus.

Titus

Titus 1:1–2—I have been sent to bring faith to those God has chosen and to teach them to know the truth that shows them how to live godly lives. This truth gives them the confidence of eternal life.

Titus 1:16—People claim they know God, but they deny him by the way they live.

Titus 2:11—The grace of God has been revealed, bringing salvation to all people.

Titus 2:14—(Jesus) gave his life to free us from every kind of sin, to cleanse us, and to make us his very own people, totally committed to doing what is right.

Titus 3:5–7—He saved us, not because of the good things we did, but because of his mercy. He washed away our sins and gave us a new life through the Holy Spirit. He generously poured out the Spirit upon us because of what Jesus Christ our Savior did. He declared us not guilty because of his great kindness. And now we know that we will inherit eternal life.

Titus 3:9–11—Do not get involved ... in quarrels and fights about obedience to Jewish laws. These kinds of things are useless and a waste of time. If anyone is causing divisions among you, give a first and second warning. After that, have nothing more to do with that person. People like that have turned away from the truth.

Hebrews

Hebrews 3:14—If we are faithful to the end, trusting God just as firmly as when we first believed, we will share in all that belongs to Christ.

Hebrews 3:19; 4:3—They were not allowed to enter his rest because of their unbelief ... Only we who believe can enter his place of rest.

Hebrews 5:9—(Jesus) became the source of eternal salvation for all those who obey him.

Hebrews 6:10–12—You have shown your love to him by caring for other Christians ... Keep right on loving others as long as life lasts, in order to make certain that what you hope for will come true. Then you will not become spiritually dull and indifferent. Instead, you will follow the example of those who are going to inherit God's promises because of their faith and patience.

Hebrews 6:18—We who have fled to him for refuge can take new courage, for we can hold on to his promise with confidence.

Hebrews 7:19—The law made nothing perfect, and now a better hope has taken its place. And that (replacing the law with Christ) is how we draw near to God.

Hebrews 7:25, 27—(Jesus) is able, once and forever, to save everyone who comes to God through him. He lives forever to plead with God on their behalf ... He does not need to offer sacrifices every day like the other high priests. They did this for their own sins first and then for the sins of the people. But Jesus did this once for all when he sacrificed himself on the cross.

Hebrews 9:10, 15—For that old system deals only with ... external regulations that are in effect only until their limitations can be corrected ... (Jesus) is the one who mediates the new covenant between God and people, so that all who are invited can receive the eternal inheritance God has promised them. For Christ died to set them free from the penalty of the sins they had committed under that first covenant.

Hebrews 9:28—(Jesus) will bring salvation to all those who are eagerly waiting for him.

Hebrews 10:10; 14–18—What God wants is for us to be made holy by the sacrifice of the body of Jesus Christ once for all time ... By that one offering he perfected forever all those whom he is making holy. And the Holy Spirit also testifies that this is so. First he says, "This is the new covenant ... I will put my laws in their hearts so they will understand them, and I will write them on their minds so they will obey them." Then he adds, "I will never again remember their sins and lawless deeds." Now when sins have been forgiven, there is no need to offer any more sacrifices.

Hebrews 10:35—Do not throw away this confident trust in the Lord, no matter what happens. Remember the great reward it brings you!

Hebrews 10:36—Patient endurance is what you need now, so you will continue to do God's will. Then you will receive all that he has promised.

Hebrews 10:39—We have faith that assures our salvation.

Hebrews 11:6—It is impossible to please God without faith. Anyone who wants to come to him must believe that there is a God and that he rewards those who sincerely seek him.

Hebrews 11:7—By (Noah's) faith he ... was made right in God's sight.

Hebrews 11:33—By faith these people ... received what God had promised them.

Hebrews 11:39—All of these people we have mentioned received God's approval because of their faith.

Hebrews 12:6, 9—The Lord disciplines those he loves ... Should we not all the more cheerfully submit to the discipline of our heavenly Father and live forever?

Hebrews 12:24—Come to Jesus, the one who mediates the new covenant between God and people.

James

James 1:12—God blesses the people who patiently endure testing. Afterward they will receive the crown of life that God has promised to those who love him.

James 1:21—Humbly accept the message God has planted in your hearts, for it is strong enough to save your souls.

James 1:26–27—If you claim to be religious but don't control your tongue, you are just fooling yourself, and your religion is worthless. Pure and lasting religion in the sight of God our Father means that we must care for orphans and widows in their troubles, and refuse to let the world corrupt us.

James 2:1, 4—How can you claim that you have faith in Christ if you favor some people more than others ... Doesn't this discrimination show that you are guided by wrong motives?

James 2:5—Aren't they (the poor) the ones who will inherit the kingdom God promised to those who love him?

James 2:12–13—You will be judged by the law of love, the law that sets you free. For there will be no mercy for you if you have not been merciful to others. But if you have been merciful, then God's mercy toward you will win out over his judgment against you.

James 2:14—What's the use of saying you have faith if you don't prove it by your actions? That kind of faith won't save anyone.

James 2:19–20—Do you still think it's enough just to believe that there is one God? Well, even the demons believe this … Faith that does not result in good deeds is useless.

James 2:22, 24—(Abraham) was trusting God so much that he was willing to do whatever God told him to do. His faith was made complete by what he did—by his actions … We are made right with God by what we do, not by faith alone.

First Peter

1 Peter 1:3–5—It is by his boundless mercy that God has given us the privilege of being born again. Now we live with a wonderful expectation because Jesus Christ rose from the dead. For God has reserved a priceless inheritance for his children … And God, in his mighty power, will protect you until you receive this salvation, because you are trusting him.

1 Peter 1:9—Your reward for trusting him will be the salvation of your souls.

1 Peter 1:18—God paid a ransom to save you.

1 Peter 1:22—You were cleansed from your sins when you accepted the truth of the Good News.

1 Peter 2:6—Anyone who believes in him will never be disappointed.

1 Peter 3:21—This is a picture of baptism, which now saves you by the power of Christ's resurrection. Baptism is not a removal of dirt from your body; it is an appeal to God from a clean conscience.

1 Peter 4:17—If even we Christians must be judged, what terrible fate awaits those who have never believed God's Good News?

1 Peter 4:19—Trust yourself to the God that made you, for he will never fail you.

1 Peter 5:5—God sets himself against the proud, but he shows favor to the humble.

1 Peter 5:10—In his kindness God called you to his eternal glory by means of Jesus Christ. After you have suffered a little while, he will restore, support, and strengthen you, and he will place you on a firm foundation.

1 Peter 5:12—The grace of God is with you no matter what happens.

Second Peter

2 Peter 1:1—Share the same faith we have, faith given to us by Jesus Christ, our God and Savior, who makes us right with God.

2 Peter 1:10–11—Work hard to prove that you really are among those God has called and chosen. Doing this, you will never stumble or fall away. And God will open wide the gates of heaven for you to enter into the eternal Kingdom of our Lord and Savior Jesus Christ.

First John

1 John 1:2—(Jesus) is the one who is eternal life.

1 John 1:7—If we are living in the light ... then we have fellowship with each other, and the blood of Jesus cleanses us from every sin.

1 John 1:9—If we confess our sins to him, he is faithful and just to forgive us and to cleanse us from every wrong.

1 John 2:3, 5—How can we be sure that we belong to him? By obeying his commandments ... Those who obey God's word really do love him. That is the way to know whether or not we live in him.

1 John 2:7, 10–11—This commandment—to love one another—is the same message you heard before ... Anyone who loves other Christians is living in the light and does not cause anyone to stumble. Anyone who hates a Christian brother or sister is living and walking in darkness. Such a person is lost.

1 John 2:17—If you do the will of God, you will live forever.

1 John 2:24–25—Remain faithful to what you have been taught from the beginning. If you do, you will continue to live in fellowship with the Son and with the Father. And in this fellowship we enjoy the eternal life he promised us.

1 John 3:10—Anyone who does not obey God's commands and does not love other Christians does not belong to God.

1 John 3:14—If we love our Christian brothers and sisters, it proves that we have passed from death to eternal life. But a person who has no love is still dead.

1 John 3:18–19—Let us stop saying we love each other; let us really show it by our actions. It is by our actions that we know we are living in the truth, so we will be confident when we stand before the Lord.

1 John 3:23–24—This is his commandment: We must believe in the name of his Son, Jesus Christ, and love one another, just as he commanded us. Those who obey God's commandments live in fellowship with him and he with them. And we know he lives in us because the Holy Spirit lives in us.

1 John 4:7–12—Let us continue to love one another, for love comes from God. Anyone who loves is born of God and knows God. But anyone who does not love does not know God—for God is love. God showed how much he loved us by sending his Son into the world so that we might have eternal life through him. This is real love. It is not that we loved God, but that he loved us and sent his Son as a sacrifice to take away our sins. Since God loved us that much, we surely ought to love each other … If we love each other, God lives in us, and his love has been brought to full expression through us.

1 John 4:15—All who proclaim that Jesus is the Son of God have God living in them.

1 John 4:16–18—God is love, and all who live in love live in God, and God lives in them. And as we live in God, our love grows more perfect. So we will not be afraid on the day of judgment, but we can face him with confidence because we are like Christ here in this world. Such love has no fear because perfect love expels all fear. If we are afraid, it is for fear of judgment, and this shows that his love has not been perfected in us.

1 John 4:21—God himself has commanded that we must love not only him but our Christian brothers and sisters, too.

1 John 5:1—Everyone who believes that Jesus is the Christ is a child of God.

1 John 5:4–5—Every child of God defeats the evil world by trusting Christ to give the victory. And the ones who win this battle against the world are the ones who believe that Jesus is the Son of God.

1 John 5:11–13—(God) has given us eternal life, and this life is in his Son. So whoever has God's Son has life; whoever does not have his Son does not have life. I write this to you who believe in the Son of God, so that you may know you have eternal life.

1 John 5:20—We are in God because we are in his Son, Jesus Christ. He is the only true God, and *He is eternal life*.

Second John

2 John verse 9—If you continue in the teaching of Christ, you will have fellowship with both the Father and the Son.

Third John

3 John verse 11—Those who do good prove that they are God's children.

Jude

Jude verse 5—(The Lord) later destroyed every one of those who did not remain faithful.

Jude verses 21–22—Live in such a way that God's love can bless you as you wait for the eternal life that our Lord Jesus Christ in his mercy is going to give you. Show mercy to those whose faith is wavering.

Revelation

Revelation 2:2–5—I know all the things you do. I have seen your hard work and your patient endurance ... You have patiently suffered for me without quitting. But I have this complaint against you. You don't love me or each other as you did at first! Look how far you have fallen ... Turn back to me.

Revelation 2:10—Remain faithful even when facing death and I will give you the crown of life.

Revelation 3:19–20—I am the one who corrects and disciplines everyone I love. Be diligent and turn away from your indifference. Look! Here I stand at the door and knock. If you hear me calling and open the door, I will come in.

Revelation 7:10—Salvation comes from our God on the throne and from the Lamb!

Revelation 7:14–17—They washed their robes in the blood of the Lamb and made them white. That is why they are standing in front of the throne of God … They will never again be hungry or thirsty, and they will be fully protected … for the Lamb who stands in front of the throne will be their shepherd. He will lead them to the springs of life-giving water.

Revelation 11:18—You will reward your prophets and your holy people, all who fear your name, from the least to the greatest.

Revelation 12:17—(The dragon) declared war against the rest of her children—all who keep God's commandments and confess that they belong to Jesus.

Revelation 16:9—Everyone was burned by this blast of heat … They did not repent and give Him glory.

Revelation 16:11—They cursed the God of heaven for their pains and sores. But they refused to repent of all their evil deeds.

Revelation 17:14—He is Lord over all lords and King over all kings, and his people are the called and chosen and faithful ones.

Revelation 19:1—Salvation is from our God. Glory and power belong to him alone.

Revelation 20:13, 15—They were all judged according to their deeds ... Anyone whose name was not found recorded in the Book of Life was thrown into the lake of fire.

Revelation 21:6–8—To all who are thirsty I will give the springs of the water of life without charge! All who are victorious will inherit all these blessings, and I will be their God, and they will be my children. But cowards who turn away from me, and unbelievers, and the corrupt, and murderers, and the immoral, and those who practice witchcraft, and idol worshipers, and all liars—their doom is in the lake that burns with fire and sulfur. This is the second death.

Revelation 22:12—I am coming soon, and my reward is with me, to repay all according to their deeds.

Revelation 22:14–15—Blessed are those who wash their robes so they can enter the gates of the city and eat the fruit from the tree of life. Outside the city are the dogs—the sorcerers, the sexually immoral, the murderers, the idol worshipers, and all who love to live a lie.

Revelation 22:17—Let the thirsty ones come—anyone who wants to. Let them come and drink the water of life without charge.

Printed in the United States
By Bookmasters